Service Innovation

Service Innovation

Anders Gustafsson, Per Kristensson,
Gary R. Schirr, and Lars Witell

Service Innovation

The Center for Services Leadership (CSL) is a research center within the W. P. Carey School of Business at Arizona State University (ASU) and an outreach arm from ASU to the business community and the global academic community. The CSL has established itself as a globally recognized authority on how to compete strategically through the profitable use of services.

The Service Research Center, CTF (ctf.kau.se) is a research center at Karlstad University, Sweden. CTF is one of the world's leading research centers with a focus on value creation through service.

First published in 2016 by
Business Expert Press, LLC
222 East 46th Street, New York, NY 10017
www.businessexpertpress.com

ISBN-13: 978-1-63157-495-5 (paperback)
ISBN-13: 978-1-63157-496-2 (e-book)

Business Expert Press Service Systems and Innovations in Business and Society Collection

Collection ISSN: 2326-2664 (print)
Collection ISSN: 2326-2699 (electronic)

Cover and interior design by Exeter Premedia Services Private Ltd., Chennai, India

First edition: 2016

10 9 8 7 6 5 4 3 2 1

Printed in the United States of America.

Abstract

The world is being shaped by service. All the world's most advanced economies are dominated by service, with many countries having more than 70 percent of their gross domestic product (GDP) generated by it. The service sector also employs the largest number of people and it is the fastest growing sector, both in number of companies and employees. The questions posed in this book are: (1) How is the service sector growing; (2) what is service innovation; (3) what are the drivers of service innovation; and (4) how can organizations innovate service in a structured way?

The book views service as the value creating activity that customers perform in their own context: The role of a company is to provide the resources and knowledge to enable value creation. Based on this view, we develop a model of service innovation. Service innovation is a multifaceted concept dependent on the purpose of the innovation. These purposes could be to: differentiate, finance, help, experience, and streamline the process or offering. In turn, these result in: brand innovation, business model innovation, social innovation, experience innovation, process innovation, and behavioral innovation, respectively. In this book, we develop guidelines for what is required from the organizational perspective, how should an organization view its customers in order to be successful, what does a service development process look like, and how to transform an organization that is goods-centric to become service or solution provider.

Despite the heightened focus on service in many business sectors, most models and theories of innovation are based on a goods perspective, assuming that the norm is a physical good. We believe that the norm is actually experiential and service based. This book addresses this mismatch of theory and practice for the benefit of those who are seeking to understand, teach, and practice service innovation.

Keywords

business, cocreation, company, creativity, customer, experience, innovation, organization, process, product, research, service, user, value creation

Contents

Preface

... the business enterprise has two—and only two—basic functions: marketing and innovation.

—Peter Drucker

Even by out-of-date traditional measures, over 70 percent of the gross domestic product (GDP) of the European Union (EU) and Sweden and over 80 percent of the GDP of the United States is service. Yet, most of the models and theories of service innovation are based on new product development for goods. This book seeks to address this mismatch of theory and practice for the benefit of those who are researching, teaching, or *practicing* service innovation.

This book is targeted to:

- Professionals involved in service innovation;
- Executives who manage those professionals;
- Executives of traditional goods firms who wish to increase service sales;
- Professionals or students seeking involvement in innovation;
- Researchers at universities or consulting firms; and
- Anyone else interested in service innovation!

The four authors of this book are university professors conducting research and teaching innovation and service marketing. Three of us are a part of the Service Research Center, CTF at Karlstad University (Sweden), a multidisciplinary center devoted to understanding service. All four of us conduct research on service innovation, read and critique current research, and teach the principles of innovation and service marketing. In addition, the four of us have been involved in service innovation as observers, consultants, and participants. We draw on both research and practice in writing this guide. We draw on evolving theory and best practice. Our goal is a book that is useful for businesspeople, consultants, researchers, and educators.

We believe that the following chapters contain guidance to the service innovator who is iterating and trying to find the right innovation process for their organization. We hope it is also useful as an indicator to consultants and researchers on topics that need further study.

Due to advances in research and innovation in practice, keeping this guide up to date will be an ongoing effort! Please feel free to contact the authors with suggestions, questions, or comments via the websites and online contacts listed in the book to aid us in this quest.

Acknowledgments

This book was supported by a grant from the Swedish Knowledge and Competence Foundation (KK-stiftelsen). We would also like to thank colleagues and friends at the Service Research Center, CTF and the Center for service leadership (CSL) for their contributions of advise and fantastic research.

In particular, we would like to thank Jim Spohrer and Haluk Demirkan for the opportunity to publish our book in the Business and Society Collection. We are also grateful to Mary Jo Bitner for her thoughtful comments and support in writing our book.

CHAPTER 1

Service as the Key Driver of Growth

The importance of physical products lies not so much in owning them as obtaining the service they render.

—Philip Kotler[1]

All marketing is service marketing.

—Vargo and Lusch[2]

There is only one boss, the customer. And he can fire everybody in the company from the chairman on down, simply by spending his money somewhere else.

—Thomas Edison

Odds are that *you*, the reader of this book, live and work in a service economy. Over half of the world's gross domestic product (GDP) and over 70 percent of the GDP of affluent nations are service related, as defined by a traditional—and we would argue restrictive—definition of service. According to the CIA *Factbook*,[3] the share of the service sector is nearly 80 percent of the GDP of the United States, United Kingdom, and France, and just over 70 percent of the GDP of most other wealthy nations, including Japan, Germany, and Sweden.

---

[1] Kotler, P. 1977. *Marketing Management: Analysis, Planning, Implementation, and Control*, 8. 3rd ed. Upper Saddle River, NJ: Prentice Hall. Emphasis added.
[2] Vargo, S.L., and R.F. Lusch. January 2004. "Evolving to a New Dominant Logic for Marketing." *Journal of Marketing* 68, no. 1, pp. 1–17; Lusch, R.F., and S.L. Vargo. 2014. *The Service-dominant Logic of Marketing: Dialog, Debate, and Directions*. USA: Routledge.
[3] CIA (Central Intelligence Agency). n.d. *The World Factbook*. www.cia.gov/library/publications/the-world-factbook/fields/2012.html

In this introduction, we review the definition of service, taking a careful look at the narrowing difference between goods and service. We prefer to use the term "service" versus "services" throughout this discussion, although at times we will use the latter term. We present the argument that all products are service.

The subjects of service innovation and service itself are both vital and understudied. If we understand service differently, it will influence both what we believe an innovation is and how it is created. We will advance the understanding of service innovation for academics and researchers but also for the men and women engaged in service innovation in organizations and their customers, working with them in cocreation. We believe that: although it is true that "in the most advanced service economies such as the USA and UK, services create up to three-quarters of the wealth and 85% of the employment ... we know little about managing innovation in this sector."[4] Service should not be treated as a special case of goods, service truly is the norm.

Service and Goods

Notice the phrase "physical products" in Kotler's quote at the beginning of the chapter. A product is a service or good offered to satisfy a customer's need or desire. Sometimes the phrase "product" is used to refer to a good or standardized service, leading people to contrast products versus services. Services are products and are, as noted, a high and growing part of gross domestic product in most economies. In this book, we will contrast goods and service and standardized service with custom service—"product" will always include service, unless identified as physical or tangible.

We will show that a tangible good can be viewed as a service. A goods-centric view, in which goods represent the products consumed by users and the ownership of goods is a goal in itself, may make service innovation difficult to understand; more importantly it may make it hard to service customer needs. To understand our modern service economy, we recommend

---

[4] Tidd, J., and F. Hull. 2003. *Service Innovation: Organizational Responses to Technological Opportunities & Market Imperatives*, ix. World Scientific Publishing Company.

a fundamental shift in focus—the answer lies not in what the product *is* but what it *does*. For example a car is primarily useful for transporting one from one point to another when needed, not for its form weight or color.

Goods or hardware remain an important part of the economy. However, if service comprises 70 to 80 percent or more of GDP in the richest countries, the production of goods is less than 30 percent of total output. In addition, goods producers increasingly package goods together with service to differentiate their offerings and create a higher value for their customers. Goods producers find that competing solely on the features of goods often leads to commoditization and basic price competition. The only remedy in this situation is an extreme innovation effort in order to keep up prices. So even products generally classified as goods become a blend of goods and service.

This book uses a modern view of service, focusing on value-creating processes rather than a type of offering. In this view, service may range from completely intangible activities, for example, a concert, to the integration of physical products, which leads to value-creating processes. We distinguish between direct and indirect service. When a physical product, such as a camera, is used, value is created for the customer through its use; hence, it is considered an indirect service, or service "waiting to happen." Direct service refer to what is usually classified as service, while physical goods or products only become service in a more modern perspective that focuses on the value-creating process itself by the customer (see Table 1.1). Direct service includes insurance, massage,

Table 1.1 Direct and indirect service

	Direct service	Indirect service
Definition	Value-creating process carried out on behalf of a customer The service is produced and consumed at the same time	Service created when a user via ability and knowledge uses something The means to the service is produced on beforehand
Example	Haircut	A ladder (a physical good) that enables a house owner to reach the roof
When is value created?	Immediately when interacting with the company	After interacting with the company and not until product is used

public transportation, car repairs, and so on. We refer to other products as "indirect service."

The Experience Matters ... a Lot

Consumers crave unique experiences: why else would they bungee jump, fly in a hot air balloon, go on holiday, or pay the equivalent of $450 per night for a cold hotel room with no shower and toilet (as in the case of the Jukkasjärvi Ice Hotel in northern Sweden)? Consumers pay for experiencing service, not just the end result. This means that smart organizations need to track the total customer experience.

Consumers, companies, and organizations purchase service today at an increasing rate. Consumers purchase theater tickets and digital music with their mobile phones; order household service; and subscribe to innumerable other service such as home alarms, grocery delivery, and so on. Personal trainers and unique travel experiences have become a priority of many customers.

When customers purchase coffee, they experience multiple types of service. The coffee's scent or aroma can brighten up a dark December morning. The coffee carton contains information on how the coffee beans were harvested (ecologically, fair-trade, etc.), which is a valuable element of the total experience for some customers. Drinking coffee is also often described as relaxing, pleasing, energizing, and an opportunity for social interaction. Even the cup that the coffee is consumed in will influence the taste and thus the experience.

Offering other products, for example, a flavored scone, together with the coffee, may increase the taste experience even further. Research shows that taste and scent experiences are linked to a person's memory, which means that a combination of coffee, sweets, and maybe a particular song has the ability to mentally transport the customer experience of sitting at a café in Rome or San Francisco. Perhaps, the staff gives advice to the customer on how to store the coffee to better preserve its freshness to allow a repeat of the aforementioned experience. The actual interaction with the coffee shop staff creates an experience that may enhance the customer's own experience, which, perhaps, in turn, prompts them to tell their friends about their experience.

The following scenarios, continuing the coffee example, illustrates why experience-promoting service is more important for the value-creating process than the product itself:

- Buying a box of coffee from the local convenience store to brew at home. Price: $0.10 per cup. (K-cup $0.50 to $0.70)
- Takeout coffee for a subway or train. Price: $1.50.
- Having a coffee with a friend in an urban café or a ubiquitous Starbucks. Price: $3 or more.
- An espresso in the Piazza Duomo square in the center of Milan, Italy. Price: $15.

The same product is purchased in all scenarios—hot coffee to drink. However, as signaled by the price, the value creating experience in each scenario varies greatly. The service is often more important to the customer than the core product and the customer's willingness to pay increases if service results in unique experiences. Howard Schultz, founder of Starbucks, has stated repeatedly that "We're not in the coffee business—we're in the experience business ..."

Even producers of products such as ventilation equipment, washing machines, or microwave ovens are in the experience business. For instance, the rotating plate in a microwave oven is really there to enhance the customer experience. An even distribution of heat can be generated without mechanical movement in the oven but some producers discovered that consumers wanted something to happen as their meal was cooking—how would they otherwise know that the oven really did its job? Consumers chose the microwave ovens with rotating plates, forcing the producers to include rotation in most of their offerings. The experience during value creation affects a customer's perceived value of a service. Customers experience a value creating service, despite purchasing a physical product! Organizations everywhere are undergoing a radical process of change resulting from a shift of focus from physical products to experiences generated for customer service.

A jogging enthusiast's ultimate running experience involves a number of products, which includes jogging shoes, transportation to the track, music, apparel, a specific training program, or information from a weather app. A service like Spotify gives a user a customized musical experience that adjusts to the pace of the run. After the run, an app like RunKeeper gives the customer the opportunity to analyze the effort with the purpose of improving performance. The same principle applies to all user experiences. Therefore, greater emphasis should be placed on experiences and on offering a solution even if the company is able to deliver only a part of it. Hardware is used to help the customer extract the intended value of a service.

In Figure 1.1, we show a continuum of service from "pure" custom and experiential service such as massages and whitewater adventure tours, to standardized packaged service such as credit cards and software, to goods used as a service such as rental cars and airline flights to what would normally be considered tangible goods—an automobile and a box of sea salt.

From left to right, the first three categories of the continuum are clearly service—that is why service constitutes such a high percentage of the economy. However, there is service everywhere in the continuum of Figure 1.1— Take a look at the "tangible goods" that some might label as "pure goods."

One of the authors recently purchased a new car, a Hyundai AWD SUV, to commute through the mountains of southwest Virginia. "Goods" features such as the all-wheel drive and five-person seating were essential, but the "service" features such as blind-spot warnings, email updates on the condition of the engine (sent by the engine computer to the owner), and a free six-month subscription to digital radio made the offering more attractive. In fact, the deciding factor for the coauthor's purchase was a 10-year, 100,000-mile warranty—a *service* promise.

Even the most basic "commodity" on the continuum, coarse sea salt, is purchased for the service it provides: The salt adheres nicely to steaks as

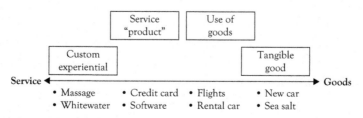

Figure 1.1 Service continuum

they are seared over an open fire or Weber grill. Furthermore, if you look for it we are sure that the producer of salt also wants to connect to you as a customer and in this process build a relationship.

The Active Customer or User

The customer plays a central part in service innovation. As will be discussed in Chapter 3, actual value-creating processes rely on active interaction between the customer and the supplier. Company offerings should be aimed at supporting the customer's own value creation.

"Customer" is an umbrella term to describe the targets of value-creating processes. The reader may replace or complement "customer" with "user" when someone other than the person using the offering is actually paying for the product or service, for example, an employer. Thus "customer" may also be interpreted as "patient" (in health care); "client" (in law or consulting); "consumer"; "member" (of an association, e.g., a trade union); "citizen" (if the supplier is a governmental agency); "pupil" or "parent" (in school), "student," "visitor"; or even "a surrounding community." This book uses "customer" as the preferred term, but insert whatever term best fits your organization and context.

In traditional scenarios, the customer passively receives something in the exchange process. In the shoe shop, the customer receives a pair of shoes and makes a payment in exchange. The customer goes to the pharmacy with a prescription from a doctor and is given medicine. In a church, the customer receives a blessing and (perhaps) pays via the collection plate or a church pledge. Imagine a theater where customers have paid and are sitting down passively receiving entertainment service while the actors represent the activity in the form of production. In this traditional view, the customer receives a prepackaged value.

This book makes a case that this logic, of passive customers and active companies, is usually erroneous. Customers act in specific contexts and use the offerings supplied to them by one or more companies. The company is tasked with supporting them in the process and should regard them as active partners working together to create value. The passive view is usually connected to which party is in control of all the events. If a company controls, such as is common in theaters, the process, the customer tends to be more passive. Value is created via the customer's activities and, customers extract what they wish from the use of different offerings.

Products represent platforms that customers use to meet their needs. A washing machine, for instance, has no value unless the customer is able to place the laundry in the machine and start it correctly. Its value can even be forfeited if clothes are washed at the wrong temperature setting or are mixed with clothes of a different color. The customers may not even need the washing machine if the job done can be solved in some other way.

Figure 1.2 is representative of the complex customer view of a service. The value of a flight is not realized at the moment of the purchase or even during the delivery of the service (the flight); in this case what the customer wanted from the service was to meet her family. The journey could start as the customer orders the journey and looks forward to meeting friends and family. If the actual trip is pleasant or even memorable it is an added bonus that adds to the customer experience. Customers can add value to their trip by bringing their own head phones, neck pillow, and bringing a good book to read during the trip. Other customers can effect the experience: if the traveler wanted to be productive, a talkative neighbor may result in a less useful experience; at other times a nice chat with another passenger may make the journey more enjoyable.

Figure 1.2 The customer experience

Source: https://medium.com/tech-doodles/latest by Kiki Schirr

Value creation is much more than a good or predetermined service produced in advance. Companies clearly must communicate and work together with their customers during the development of new service.

What Does the Term "Service" Really Mean?

The term "service" has changed during the past century. For a long time, service was treated as a residual entry in a country's financial accounts (found in a "miscellaneous" column also referred to as unproductive labor) and regarded as a less valuable entity since it was not exportable. Today, however, service is the backbone of a modern economy. Goods have become commodities and service is the key product differentiator.

Let's contrast three different perspectives of service that are in use today. The first perspective is that service comprises offerings from a special group of companies and organizations, or defined subsidiaries. In this perspective, service output is to the sum of the output created by firms and organizations in defined service sectors including for instance travel, finance, and insurance. Service sectors are defined using classification codes from organizations including NACE—codes used for economic activities in the European Union, the United Nations (UN), the Organization for Economic Co-operation, and Development (OECD), as well as the CIA figures cited earlier.

This classification perspective is useful to compare economies or track changes over time, but does not add much insight at the micro or individual level of analysis. If 50 percent or more of Volvo Trucks', Ericsson's, or GE's revenue consists of service, are they still product firms? The answer may be "yes" according to this traditional perspective. If a staff canteen run by a goods firm is sold off to someone outside the firm, the goods firm becomes more productive in that the firm uses less staff to produce more. This shows that the traditional perspective is a very crude way to measure.

The second service perspective is based on the features contained in an offering. If it is intangible and produced at the same time as it is consumed, this perspective regards it as a service, while it is regarded as a product if it can be inventoried and standardized. One could say, somewhat facetiously, that dropping a service on one's foot does not hurt, as opposed to products. This service perspective is based on the so-called intangibility, heterogeneity, inseparability, and perishability or IHIP criteria (see Table 1.2). IHIP works well in a theoretical or an educational setting, but one quickly encounters situations in which it does not correspond well with reality.

As shown in Table 1.2, the IHIP model suffers from a number of uncertainties. It needs revamping in order to provide knowledge and insight of optimal service handling in an organization. In addition to

Table 1.2 IHIP—a traditional service perspective

IHIP	Definition	Our comments—A new way of thinking
Intangibility	Service is intellectual and intangible, for example, a mortgage loan.	A service (e.g., a mortgage loan) often carries a material consequence (e.g., a house). A material purchase is also often made for its intangible value (e.g., living somewhere). Whether something is tangible or not is also relatively insignificant since the customer is looking for value and does not care if the offering is tangible or not.
Heterogeneity	Service varies from time to time, for example, a hotel stay.	The way in which value is perceived from one point to another also applies to products and does not thereby distinguish service from physical products. If heterogeneity is the definition of service, it is possible to view homogeneity as the definition of products. This implies that standardization is the goal of production; however, the actual goal, which applies to both products and service, should be personalization.
Inseparability	Production and consumption of service is indistinguishable.	The most important aspect to take into account is that the customer (the user) always takes part in production (of value). Everything else implies an "inward outward" paradigm. Maximizing the potential and assisting the customer in personally customizing the value creation should be the goal of every organization.
Perishability	Physical products are tangible while intellectual service cannot be stored.	Whether or not offerings disappear over time shifts the focus from the important issue, which is how long the generated value survives. Focus should lie on the latter. Warehousing and inventory are hardly a financial advantage to companies.

the issues outlined in the table—leasing a car, for instance, would be considered a service, although most would probably regard the car itself as a good. A car, however, can also be customized according to preferences on purchase, which, according to IHIP, is a service characteristic.

One of the most important values of a product (e.g., Apple's) is its brand—specifically a service according to IHIP—and in this scenario, a service defines the price of a product. The topic concerning the difficulty in standardizing service (the "H" in IHIP) brings the concept of lending rates into discussion, which should be one of the more standardized offerings on a market, while the qualities of two equivalent cars sometimes vary considerably.

The aforementioned example illustrates the difficulty in defining service. In order to help organizations provide competitive offerings, a new outlook is required, which is an important theme in this book. As previously mentioned, the focal point is the value created by the customer in use. Therefore, the third and final service perspective, stipulates that the value-creating processes, often a combination of several goods and service providers, define the provided service. It is a value-creation perspective and focus lies on what facilitates value cocreated by the customer.

From the value-creation perspective, every product is a service, direct or indirect, since it creates opportunities for value-creating processes! A service refers to providing help to someone to achieve a certain goal; hence, every product can be regarded as a service. In the words of Clayton Christensen, a customer "hires" a good or service to do a job.[5]

A hotel stay is the direct service of providing a comfortable place to sleep and reside. A TV provides the indirect service of entertainment or information on what is happening in the world. A mechanical robot provides us with the indirect service of carrying out technical and difficult tasks in a cost-effective manner. The service itself is the value-creating process that appears on use.

---

[5] Christensen, C.M., S.D. Anthony, G. Berstell, and D. Nitterhouse. 2007. "Finding the Right Job for Your Product." *MIT Sloan Management Review* 48, no. 3, pp. 38–49.

Value-Creating Processes, Customer Experience, and Context

We consider *value-creating processes* to be the golden goal of service innovation. We would like to introduce additional key terms—value, customer experience, and context—needed to understand what value-creating processes really are.

Value refers to fulfilling the goals a customer wants to achieve in exchange for a reasonable amount of resources. Value is created when the goals are achieved via activities that take place between the customer and the company in some kind of interaction. The customer usually performs the majority of the actual activities, while the company supplies the resources. For example, the company produces the lawn mower but the customer puts it into use when cutting the grass.

Customer or user activities are a key part of the value-creating processes. A resource (washing machine, the detergent, and the knowledge of how to start it) has no value without customer activities; no clothes will be washed without a customer placing the clothes in the washing machine. Value can, however, be created without company participation if the customer, for instance, buys a used washing machine from another person; goes to a drycleaner; borrows the neighbors' washing machine; or washes the clothes in the sink. In this case, value is not produced by firm activities, but solely by customers. Firms and organizations provide propositions for value creation but from how companies are marketing their products, one often gets the feeling that they perceive value as something that is produced in their manufacturing process.

Customer experience refers to the feelings and thoughts that occur in connection with, or after, the execution of activities. For instance, a coffee shop could also be described as a social icebreaker, a tool that enables social interaction and creates experiences both during the chat and afterwards. In the previously mentioned washing machine example, experience most likely occurs after the activities, when one is putting on newly washed clothes, feeling clean and invigorated. The value-creating processes are immediate and the experience is represented by the feelings that occur within the individual.

Another example used to further clarify what we mean by customer experience is gardening activities—grass cutting (an activity) is performed with the help of a lawn mower (a resource offered by an organization) driven by gasoline (another resource). Value is created when the lawn mower is running and being used, and afterwards, when sitting on the porch looking at the children running around on the newly mowed lawn. Feelings content follow the scent of newly cut grass and the look of a tended garden.

Customer experiences are very much governed by previous experiences and expectations. Recall how it felt when acquiring a new complex skill, for example, learning to drive, compared to how it feels after having acquired it. Experience is a double-edged sword in a development process—knowing how something works enables quick acquisition of knowledge, but the same knowledge will also limit creativity. This since we know how things are done! Even a review of a service by a trusted friend can frame how a service is perceived. The reason for these differences is that our brains work on a different script when we are learning something new compared with the routine behavior we display after we master something.

Finally, *context* or environment is the core component in the assessment of value and perception of how good or bad the resulting experience is. The previous coffee example illustrated the impact the environment has: a cup of coffee in Milan is perceived (and valued) differently from the same cup somewhere else. In a humorous experiment by *The Washington Post*, world-famous violinist Joshua Bell played incognito in the underground station L'Enfant Plaza in Washington, DC. It was filmed using hidden cameras and is now available on YouTube. In total, almost 1,100 people passed by as Bell was playing, yet only seven stopped to listen to him. Of these seven, only one recognized him. Bell was given $32 for his near 45-minute-long performance (excluding $20 from the one who recognized him). Compare this to the night before, when he made considerably more money playing the exact same repertoire in a sold-out and well-established concert hall.

Resources, Knowledge, and Skills

From this discussion, we can identify the main components of a service. The first is resources, which comprises offerings from companies and organizations, as well as knowledge and activities carried out by the customer. These resources typically need to be integrated in some fashion. Imagine hosting a party—resources are available in the form of a barbeque grill, furniture, music, beer, wine and crisps, and so on. One may know the best way to cook the food and arrange the party. As a result, value creation occurs, for example, enjoyment, when all these resources are integrated both during and after the party. The last part of the service regards the experiences that occur, which is a result of the value-creating process. Schematically creating a model that delineates the main components of a service may look like Figure 1.3.

Every value-creating process includes customers experience—sometimes significant and sometimes so minute that it is not given any thought. The experiences span the entire human emotional spectrum and may therefore range from well-being, joy, security, and relaxation to sadness, irritation, stress, and aggression.

Value-creation processes vary by industry. The financial industry is concerned with growth and security, the hotel and restaurant industry with customer treatment, and the industrial sector with competitiveness and productivity. The consumer markets' value-creating processes often embody cost and time saving, learning, security, well-being, entertainment, experiences, socializing, or autonomy (being able to independently maintain order). In business markets, the processes are even more driven by cost and time savings, competitiveness, or production capacity, although this sector also contains experience elements. A brand may be perceived

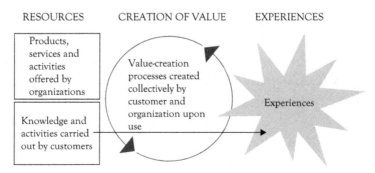

Figure 1.3 Resources create opportunities for value creating processes that result in experiences

as more reliable, more efficient and service-oriented, more fun, or more socially conscious than the competitor.

The value-creating processes require resources, including product offerings. Also, the ever-important but oft-forgotten knowledge and skills are required by the customer in order to use products and service the right way. Spaghetti that is boiled for half an hour does not taste too good, and a computer feature that is not used because the customer does not understand it is not very beneficial. Knowledge and abilities found among employees also represent important resources. A pint of beer often tastes better in combination with, for instance, peanuts or crisps, and a festival organizer relies on nearby hotel chains to provide an attractive overall experience.

Customers do not purchase goods and service because they are interested in ownership—rather, customers purchase products because they are prerequisites for value-creating processes. Service leads to service and goods lead to service. A customer does not go to the hospital to see a doctor, but, rather, to get well. A customer or student does not go to university to listen to a professor, but to get relevant education for an interesting job. Getting well is a service that most likely entails experiences of health, and getting an interesting job entails experiences in the form of self-esteem, meaningfulness, and skillsets.

The Book's Terms, Concepts, and Content

As noted earlier, the word customer is used as an umbrella term for every potentially innovation user. A customer could be a company, consumer, museum visitor, parent, and so on. Another commonly used term is offering or products, which refers to the goods and service offered on a market by a company or organization. These are often combined by the customer with other goods and service—a good, for example, a mobile phone, is not used in isolation and does not generate any value until it is used together with the SIM card service, which enables connecting to an operator, a network, and so on.

There is an extensive research literature on how companies can base their strategies on the perspectives of the customers and focus on value-creating processes. The key realization in this chapter is fairly simple and can be summarized with Professor Theodore Levitt's famous statement:

People don't want to buy a quarter-inch drill. They want a quarter-inch hole![6]

Companies usually agree with this sentiment; yet markets are still segmented into the type of drill and price, and the market share assessment is based on drills but not on holes! Comparisons between competitors are based on drills and new functions are developed based on what is technically possible but not on demand, in the belief that it leads to better prices and larger market shares. It is indeed easy to improve the products in a way that leads to better technical performance, although it is often irrelevant to the customers. Segmenting markets according to the type of customer is not much better either. We can speak in terms of business customers consisting of small, average, and large companies, or pigeonhole consumers into age, sex, or lifestyle. Companies then try to identify customer needs in said segments and try to develop products that meet those needs.

The market structure, from the customer's perspective, is very simple: They just need to get things done, just as Theodore Levitt stated. Taking his position even further, however, proves that even he was not entirely correct: people probably do not want a hole either—perhaps they just want to put a painting on the wall that they can enjoy! When people need to get a job done, they will find one or more products that either in isolation or integration is able to meet this need.

A company's objective is therefore to understand what jobs the customer needs to perform and reflect on what part the firm plays in order to make life easier for the customer. This is specifically the objective if working at a company or in a public sector organization: the way in which you may support the customer's process.

The authors believe that *all products are service*. In the words of Dr. Christensen, consumers hire products to get a job done. If you cannot fully accept this view that all products are service, you might still acknowledge that this approach may be "close enough." In an economy that is 70 to 80 percent service even by traditional definition, with many

---

[6] Christensen, C.M., S. Cook, and T. Hall. 2005. "Marketing Malpractice." *Harvard Business Review* 83, no. 12, pp. 74–83.

of the remaining goods having a large service component, is it not far more logical to focus on innovation from the service perspective than the traditional way? If nothing else, it can provide a fresh perspective on how your firm develops its offerings.

In the following sections we aim to cover some of the underlying principles in this book.

Innovation in Cocreated Service

Most of the models and processes for new product development are based on production of goods. Similarly, most of the research on theories and models of "new product development" in leading academic journals of marketing, management, and innovation focuses on innovation of goods.[7] Service is just a special case that these product based models are applied to and that may not always work well.

This book focuses on the principles, theories, and practices of service innovation. In the discussion all products are service, we have pointed out that (1) customers hire service and goods to perform a job, (2) users cocreate service when performing the job, and (3) the experience of the service is a key part of the value-creating process. Research on service innovation must therefore identify the customer job, focus on the process of value cocreation, and achieve an understanding of the customer experience.

Service innovation and service entrepreneurship are a huge force in a world economy dominated by service. How have companies such as YouTube, Facebook, Instagram, Snapchat, Skype, and Spotify become worth several billion dollars within only a few years? They have achieved valuations that took traditional goods-based companies such as General Electric, Philips, IBM, and Ford decades to obtain.[8]

---

[7] Page, A.L., and G.R. Schirr. 2008. "Growth and Development of a Body of Knowledge: 16 Years of New Product Development Research, 1989–2004." *Journal of Product Innovation Management* 25, no. 3, pp. 233–48.

[8] This book uses the terms "company" and "organization" interchangeably. Most of the time, the content is applicable to both companies and nonprofit or governmental organizations. In Chapter 6, we refer specifically to companies and therefore use that term exclusively.

The goal of this book is to advance the understanding of service innovation. Key questions that this book addresses include:

- How is new service created?
- Are there different types of service innovations?
- How does service innovation differ from traditional new product development processes based on goods?
- How can organizations develop better service in the future?

Answers to these questions constitute the body of knowledge of this book, which outlines how to work with service innovation in your company or organization in a structured manner.

Service Innovation—The Value Experienced by the Customer

Service innovation refers to a new value experienced by a user (i.e., a customer, patient, user, client, etc.) via a new or improved process in which the user is a cocreator. Online and social service such as Spotify and Facebook have increased the availability of music anywhere at any time, the opportunities for communication with friends and associates, and the ease of acquiring new knowledge. In hindsight, it is not surprising that these three service firms have grown into very large enterprises in a short time. Service innovations have focused on improving life for users by offering faster, better and, in some cases, more environmentally friendly ways of transporting groceries from the store to one's home, running bank errands, cleaning the house, or doing gardening activities.

Service innovation may consist of new ways of coordinating value creation. For some jobs, customers use resources from multiple companies in order to meet their needs. Taking a holiday trip, for instance, may require contacting: travel agencies, hotels, transport companies, stores, restaurants, and so on. Helping a user coordinate these choices makes the decisions easier and likely produces a more enjoyable experience. There have been a number of service innovations from companies collaborating with other actors in establishing systems to solve customers' problems and simplify the process for them.

Similarly, service providers may innovate by realizing that the scarcest resource of many customers is time. Some kitchen renovation companies now schedule remodeling to be completed while the customer is on a family holiday. Some airports allow car owners to hand in their cars at check-in for cleaning, servicing, or both, which are completed by the time the owner returns. Such solutions emphasizing convenience require collaboration in order to jointly offer the new value creating service innovation. Such collaboration or partnering between service providers is a recurrent theme of service innovation.

Another example of service innovation is innovation in the cocreation experience—innovation seeking to create unique or enjoyable experiences. As noted earlier, consumers pay to jump of bridges (bungee), fly in balloons, and stay in very rustic accommodations. Additional examples of this type of service innovation of experience are cooking a meal with star chefs. The cooking participant pays far more for the privilege of assisting with the meal preparation than the cost of sipping wine in the restaurant awaiting the same meal to be served.

Even branding can be considered a service innovation: Customers may feel trendier and more at ease doing boring spreadsheet manipulations in a high-end coffee shop if they are using an Apple computer than on a Lenovo or Dell. "Cult brands" such as Nike, Apple, Adidas, Harley Davidson, Ikea, and MINI affect the user experience and even the self-identity of the loyal customers.

Service innovations do not take place only in the consumer or B2C organizations—B2B firms are also working on service innovation. The abbreviation B2C is short for business to consumer and consequently B2B indicates business to business. Coping with foreign competition and "commoditization" of goods forces a focus on service. Returning to a key concept from the Introduction: customers do not want to own 100 computers in a computing center; they want to use a specified amount of computing power. B2B firms focus on service innovation to assist the customer in cost savings and sales increases.

Another example of innovation in cocreation or coproduction is the effort by health care providers to promote more patient involvement in their treatment. Social innovations—that is, innovations in the nonprofit sector with the purpose of helping others—also necessarily focus on the experience of clients being served.

Industrial companies speak in terms of delivering solutions that range from overtaking factory operations and maintaining intermediate warehouses to performing preventive maintenance operations. Some industrial companies have taken this concept so far that the term "servitization," "service infusion" or "solution selling"—a process we will discuss in detail in Chapter 6—has appeared on the agenda.

Service innovation involves far more actors than just the organization's formal development or product management staff. Service innovation often happens outside the research and development (R&D) lab. Organizational leaders, marketers, product owners, salespeople, frontline staff, and logistics—almost every resource in an organization works with service innovation. Actors external to the organization, such as designers, start-up incubators, company advisers, consulting companies, and definitely customers, may all be involved in service innovation.

The ideas and processes discussed in this book should be useful to all of the participants and stakeholders in service innovation. We believe that many individuals currently involved in service innovation will benefit from this discussion of practices, procedures, and theories of service innovation.

Identifying Customer Needs

Service innovation begins by identifying user needs. This shift in focus from what is technically possible to what the customer needs leads to a number of consequences in terms of how a development project in an organization is carried out. Development may move from the laboratory to where the customer operates. Multiple departments—again including R&D, customer service, business development, marketing, and logistics—are involved in service innovation. Other companies that can contribute to value creation for the customer may be asked to participate. In this "outside-in" or "open" approach, the customer and his or her activities serve as the starting point for service innovation.

What job does the customer want to be done? In a service economy, the focus of innovation should not be to invent a new mousetrap, but on developing the most effective procedure to control rodents in a household; not on adding chrome to a car, but on more efficient and safer transportation solutions for the customer. This suggests a total-solution or service innovation approach to making a company more competitive.

The company Tetra Pak actually refers to a type of customer efficiency improvement that could be achieved by removing a part of the customers' hardware to allow them to focus more directly on the production process. This implies a solution that perhaps does not consist of increased machinery investments, but of what actually takes place in the value-creating processes.

Dr. Philip Kotler established planning and thought processes for launching new products. He noted, as shown in the introduction to this chapter, already in 1977 that:

The importance of physical products lies not so much in owning them as obtaining the service they render.[9]

Service innovation involves developing value-creating processes, improving value-creating processes, or both. So, while product innovation involves developing a new offering, typically a physical good, service innovation involves developing resources that, when being used, render the customer value creation. The difference in terms of semantics might not sound as particularly large, but as discussed at length in the Introduction, requires a new mindset about service and correspondingly about service innovation.

Many companies now face the challenge of constant innovation in order to compete in the marketplace. They may be hindered by using strategies, processes, methods, and guidelines developed for new product development of goods. This book is built on a body of knowledge acquired from working with companies involved in service innovation and in research on the courses of action that companies around the world have used for successful service innovation.

Active Customers, Innovative Customers

It is essential to view users and customers as actively involved in the coproduction or cocreation of a service. Viewing the customer as an

---

[9] Kotler, P. 1977. *Marketing Management: Analysis, Planning, Implementation, and Control*, 8. 3rd ed. Upper Saddle River, NJ: Prentice Hall. Emphasis added.

active partner leads to a number of new service innovation opportunities for companies and organizations. Making the service offered by an organization transparent and sufficiently compatible with other products and service will allow the customer to customize the organization's offers to further meet specific needs. For example, Coca-Cola™ has developed new vending machines that allow users to customize flavor combinations in their soft drinks. Coca-Cola has also obtained ideas for new soft drinks by observing the combinations that users create in those customizable vending machines.

Consider Apple's products: customers customize their iPhone or iPad experience with their selection of apps and may even develop their own apps. A customer is motivated to buy other Apple products in part to share the customization and apps already installed in the Apple product owned. Another example is clothing articles where the customers may choose colors to match their personal style and combine them with other articles of clothing they already own, happening at stores like Uniqlo, which is popular with young consumers in Europe and the United States.

Value creation is much more than a good or predetermined service produced in advance. Companies clearly must communicate and work together with their customers during the development of new service offerings.

Cases of Service Innovation

The purpose of this book is to help organizations succeed in service innovation. It is intended to provide you with tools for success in service innovation by contributing with the following:

- Descriptions of different types of service innovations and their effects.
- Examples of successful and unsuccessful service innovations.
- Identification of critical mechanisms in the innovation process that organizations have to manage.
- Summaries of important research on service innovation.

A service innovation denotes new value-creating processes that occur on the customer's behalf upon use (or shortly thereafter), which result in enhanced experiences. This is a very important foundational concept since it means that companies and organizations are able to create service innovations in many more ways than by simply launching a new type of offering. Innovation can mean new, improved, or simply different.

An interesting example of innovation in an old, and actually declining, business is the free tabloid newspapers *Metro*, distributed throughout Sweden, and *RedEye*, in Chicago, Illinois—their service innovation breaks the oft-cited prerequisites for successful product development, as by most measures it would be hard to describe the products as new, better, or targeting a growing market:

- Newspapers have existed for more than 200 years, in standard or tabloid format.
- Neither *Metro* nor *RedEye* was the first to conceive the idea of handing out a newspaper at central public transportation hubs (The Swiss newspaper *20 minuten* was ahead of *Metro* in Europe and *RedEye* was created a decade after *Metro*).
- Nor was the business model of either publication based on launching a newspaper that was "better" or higher in perceived quality than others (Swedish papers *Dagens Nyheter* and *Svenska Dagbladet* rate far higher than *Metro* in terms of quality, as do the two existing Chicago daily newspapers compared to *RedEye*).

So what did these two free newspapers do well? These publications provide customers with important service innovations and experiences:

- They are free newspapers, providing daily news to those who do not subscribe to other papers and an alternative for those who do.
- The newspapers are small and easy to read in cramped spaces on mass transit rides.
- The newspapers offer the value-creating process of reading where one would otherwise just be sitting down waiting at a transit spot or riding a train or bus—offering reading as a means of passing time.

- Advertisements and subscriptions are generally a newspaper's main revenue source. The problem with subscriptions is that the distribution costs are enormous. Handing out newspapers at central locations such as subway entrances for free lowers the distribution cost dramatically while simultaneously increasing the number of readers and advertising revenue. (A former executive of *The Tribune*, who was involved in the *RedEye* launch, told one of the authors that the "paper became profitable the day we stopped charging for it.")

Another interesting innovation example from a nonglamorous industry is the company Off2off, which received the 2013 award for best service innovation in Sweden. Off2off helps large organizations manage and distribute functional surpluses, taking care of things that are too good to throw away. Off2off collects office furniture and supplies to sell to other offices. Off2off tries to match access, need, and demand by acquiring assets that are no longer needed in the public sector (e.g., visitor chairs at a municipal administration) and selling them to other public administrations where a need exists (e.g., county councils). The value-creating processes that occur do not just lead to effectiveness for both parties (one party purchases products at a low price and the other gets paid for something that would otherwise be thrown away or stored), but also to ecofriendly values in terms of reduced consumption and recycling, energy emissions upon transportation, and material consumption. Off2off also generates value in the form of reduced purchase needs and more efficient delivery (since the product an organization wants to buy has already been produced). The main problem with the innovation is that it is a process type innovation rather than a brand innovation; it makes the process of reuse easier. Process innovations are generally easy to copy.

Metro, RedEye, and Off2off may be regarded as radical or possibly disruptive innovations (more information on this topic, as well as other types of innovations, is available in Chapter 2). The reason why most people seldom know of several different service innovations is because the innovations are seldom radical but, rather, incremental, that is, they consist of smaller changes in a system, for example, combining existing offerings in a new way. Incremental improvements seem faster and easier in service innovation. The cumulative effect of multiple incremental innovations can be radical.

One reason for the incremental nature of service innovation is that it takes time to implement or spread the innovations. For instance, Spotify's founders describe how they, for several years, were working on solving the copyright issue with record companies. If a service innovation is too radical, it may cause too great an increase in adoption time and the customers may perceive the innovation itself as too complex. Since the focus of service innovation lies on new value-creating processes, it often becomes counterproductive and problematic if the innovation leads to excessive transitional demand.

Service Innovation—A New Logic

When people talk of recent innovations, they generally focus on "goods" such as the Apple iPad or iPhone, and do not necessarily focus on the integration with other services that actually make the Apple products special. One might wonder why companies like Snapchat, Ikea, Skype, or H&M are less frequently mentioned when talking about innovation, as they are also wonderfully successful and are a part of our lives. Somehow pure service innovation does not seem to attract as much attention.

Ikea's service innovation is based on offering designer furniture at a low price. It is able to do this by letting the customer prepare his or her purchase by browsing their catalog and website, after which the customer visits the store and acts as an employee at the warehouse (fetching the product), as a carrier (bringing the product home), and also as a fitter (assembling the product). Skype is a service innovation that enables low-cost, and sometimes even free, calls all over the world without even having to know a telephone number. H&M has invented a model that entails low production costs and recognized design. The service innovations of all companies mentioned are based on the same concept: They are built on a profound understanding of what the customer wants, for example, cost saving, design, availability, time saving, and user-friendliness.

Traditional innovation processes start inside a company or organization. It consists of a new product-development process framework and employees and resources committed to innovation. We refer to this as an inside-out approach or "technology push." There is no guarantee that an inside-out or technology push innovation becomes a market success. According to the so-called performance indicator "idea attrition rate," only one in 15 launched ideas ever become financial successes for a company. Steve Jobs (Apple's former chief executive officer) once said: "*You've got to start with the customer experience and work back to the technology—not the other way round.*"[10] In the case of development processes, however, it is easy to become overly concerned with technical possibilities and consequently forget the value-creating process the user is interested in given the context. Steve Jobs is sometimes mentioned as an excuse for not involving the customers. Apple's success over the years is proof that this strategy can work—but the process requires the customer understanding exhibited by Steve Jobs. Often a company acquires knowledge of the customers' value-creating processes by collaborating with them.

A service innovation process is characterized by being organized as an outside-in approach, that is, the reverse logic. The differences between the most critical components of the production and service innovation process are shown in Table 1.3.

As shown in the table, ideas of new value-creating processes are the backbone of service innovations, in contrast to new product-development processes of goods, which often refer to new technology or a new way of using resources. Key assets in terms of product innovation are, as a consequence of the previously mentioned components, often patents, while the equivalent components for service innovations instead pertain to knowledge of needs that have not yet been met. While patents lead to secrecy and closed innovation processes, the service innovation processes are more open. This is required in order to eventually be able to invite customers and other requisite partners to allow the service innovation to become a value-creating process.

---

[10] Kristensson, P. 2012. *New Forms of Support for Open and User-Driven Innovation Management*, 36. Pro Inno Europe.

Table 1.3 Differences between goods innovation and service innovation

Process	Goods innovation	Service innovation
Initiation of the innovation process	New usage of an existing resource, new technology	An idea of a value-generating process that is not realized (either at all or well enough)
Key asset	Patent	Knowledge of latent needs (that are not met)
Degree of transparency in the development processes	Closed	Open
View of need	Needs are noncomplex. They can be created via campaigns.	Needs are complex and difficult to communicate. They are often latent.
View of resources	Resources primarily consist of tangible assets that the organization has control over	Resources are primarily represented by knowledge and human ability both in and outside the organization
Participants in the development process	Primarily the R&D and cross-functional teams	Partners and customers. Participants from different functions across the organization
Marketing	Persuasion, push	Dialog, pull
End result	New product or service	New value-generating process (which is a service)

The Remainder of This Book

This book is based on experiences and knowledge gathered from scientific studies carried out both by our colleagues and us. For readability, we have chosen not to use inline references as is customary in scientific reports or journal articles—instead we have included them at the end of each chapter. References to direct quotes, however, are denoted with a footnote. We believe that this increases readability and our understanding is that those interested in this book are primarily looking for knowledge related to the results of different studies and not so much in how a certain study was carried out.

Several published management books have been based solely on single cases or experiences from a particular managerial position. Our book distinguishes itself by basing its content on experiences and knowledge from numerous projects run by market-leading companies, both in Sweden and the United States.

The book is structured as follows:

- Chapter 1 is an introduction to the concept of service.
- Chapter 2 presents a background on innovation in service and introduces a new model for service innovation.
- Chapter 3 outlines the service innovation-driven organization and describes mindsets and methods needed in organizations that are trying to understand value creation.
- Chapter 4 describes the service innovation processes and their various phases.
- Chapter 5 outlines different ways that customers can participate in developing service innovations; it also discusses lead users and other methods used for customer involvement.
- Chapter 6 focuses on what is popularly referred to as servitization or service infusion and outlines how goods firms may follow a service logic.
- Chapter 7, which is the final chapter, summarizes the book and re-emphasizes what we believe are key activities in successful service innovation.

Action questions are listed at the end of each chapter to encourage the reader to reflect on various issues connected to the business they work in (or wish to work in). We believe the connection between theory and practice is key to understanding what service innovation is and how we can create organizations that develop service innovations of the future. The key ingredient in these organizations consists of individuals who are creative and have the knowledge and skills to think about service.

Action questions for the service innovator:

- What service(s) does your organization offer?
- What service innovations is your organization currently working on?

- What "jobs" do your customers use your offerings for in order to create value? Or what is your organization's role in the customer value-creation process?
- In your opinion, what values are created (to the customer or user) as a result of the service offered by your organization?

Sources of inspiration for this chapter include two of the most influential studies in the field:

Vargo, S.L., and R.F. Lusch. 2004. "Evolving to a New Dominant Logic for Marketing." *Journal of Marketing* 68, no. 1, pp. 1–17.

Grönroos, C., and P. Voima. 2013. "Critical Service Logic: Making Sense of Value Creation and Co-creation." *Journal of the Academy of Marketing Science* 41, no. 2, pp. 133–50.

The following are important sources of inspiration in terms of subject matter articles related to the actual development process of value creation:

Christensen, C.M., S.D. Anthony, G. Berstell, and D. Nitterhouse. 2007. "Finding the Right Job for Your Product." *MIT Sloan Management Review* 48, no. 3, pp. 38–49.

Meyer, C., and S. Andre. 2007. "Understanding Customer Experience." *Harvard Business Review* 85, no. 2, pp. 116–26.

Kim, W.C., and R. Mauborgne. 2004. "Value Innovation: The Strategic Logic of High Growth." *Harvard Business Review* 82, no. 7–8, pp. 172–80.

CHAPTER 2

What Is Service Innovation?

If you want something new, you have to stop doing something old or if you do what you did you get what you got.

—Peter Drucker

In this chapter, we describe service innovation and what sets it apart from new product development focused on goods or hardware. We will show that service innovation involves a wider and more holistic approach to innovation, comprising process, experience, social aspects, and behavioral and business models or in essence what creates value for customers.

What service do you think of when hearing the term "service innovation"? Many people find this question very difficult and we do receive replies like the concept of "lean" or Internet banking. If you were asked about innovations in physical products many possibilities such as smart phones, mobile devices, mountain bikes, or electric cars would likely come to mind. Why does it seem easier to think of product innovations than service innovations? When we informally asked colleagues they tended to recall branded services such as McDonald's, Ikea, Starbucks, Southwest Air, Google, or Facebook. The question then is service innovation synonymous with a brand? What are the characteristics of service innovation?

This chapter covers these questions and more in the context of describing service innovation and how it differs from the innovation of physical products. We review and categorize different types of service innovations and illustrate them with examples including Ikea and Skype.

Preview of Action Questions

Each chapter of this book concludes with a list of "action questions" for the service innovator. The authors believe that it may be helpful to the reader to preview a couple of selected questions to consider while reading the chapter:

- What other products and services do your customers use along with your offerings to do their "job" or create value?
- What is your customer experience: how do users feel when they use your product to create value?
- Can you envision a "business model innovation" or alternative revenue model in the market your organization serves?

A New Outlook on Value

Viewing services—not physical products—as a platform for innovation leads to a focus on value-creating processes for customers (see Figure 2.1).

We call this service logic: Goods and services are valued for providing the prerequisites for value creation during usage. From this viewpoint,

Figure 2.1 The value of "being in nature" is facilitated by purchasing running shoes

the term "service" becomes a perspective of value and not simply a cat-egory of offerings. Thus, the service is the value that arises from using various offerings. The customer contributes the knowledge, skills, and activities that facilitate the realization of value using the prerequisites. A customer often uses goods and services in combination to create value. A mobile phone is supposed to be used in a particular way depending on the subscription plan—the number of free text messages or the num-ber of gigabytes of data allows shape one's communication with family, friends, and colleagues. It is not constructive to regard goods or services as separate entities since they are, quite simply, resources the customer uses to create value. Some companies believe that their products alone create value. However, user resources for value creation in addition to goods and services also include knowledge, skills, and activities. Customers also know the type of solution that makes best sense for them in their context.

Service logic is based on understanding how our resources in the form of products, activities, and interactions lead to customer value during use in a certain context. The notion that value arises during use requires com-panies to adjust their way of thinking and their actions to create business models in which value creation can be facilitated, as early as in the develop-ment process. Let us look at a few brief examples. The value of ice cream is not realized until it is eaten. Resources required for value creation are, aside from the ice cream itself, a wafer and perhaps a park bench to sit on and a newspaper to read. All these resources affect the experience. If it starts to rain while sitting on the park bench, the experienced value of the ice cream will be affected. A narrow focus on the physical product may miss a key factor in a customer experience or opportunities. If you are narrowly focused on the ice cream you may miss the chance to create PinkBerry! PinkBerry builds a concept that includes frozen yoghurt and fresh fruit.

The fact that a product's value is created during use, and not in the manufacturing process or the store where it is perhaps sold, shifts the focus from the traditional product attributes to the customers' activities and experiences using the product. A car provides the means for trans-portation. Instead of having companies concentrate on the average fuel consumption and various features, focus can be shifted to designing "the right-sized car for the most added value." Transport solutions are thus perceived differently and the user's values and needs shape this decision as opposed to objective product attributes. Some customers value traveling in a quiet vehicle highly while others prioritize low cost or ecofriendliness. Maybe, a car is the best solution for part of the transportation need while other means (e.g., train or airplane) are better for other parts.

Dr. Christensen and his colleagues provided insight into innovation driven by understanding the "job" of the offering, when studying milkshake consumption at a fast food chain.[1] From detailed observation the researchers found two distinct jobs for milk shakes in the morning and in the evening: (1) early morning commuters found milk shakes comforting on their morning journey and enjoyed consuming for the entire trip, and (2) parents rewarded (or bribed) their children with milk shakes in the evening—same product but different jobs. The jobs suggested different innovations. For the morning commuters, who want the shake to last the whole commute and add interest to the journey: "Make the shake even thicker, so it would last longer, and swirl in tiny chunks of fruit ... [to] ... make the commute more interesting ... adding a dimension of unpredictability and anticipation to their monotonous morning routine" (p. 39). In contrast, for the evening consumption by children, it might make sense to make the shakes sweeter and thinner, so that the parents do not have to wait around the restaurant so long for the kids to finish!

Focusing on service logic and value creation changes the perception of innovation. An innovation is traditionally regarded as new technology or attributes connected to a product. Service innovation, based on service logic and value creation, encompasses not only the development of new and "improved" services or outcomes, but also the knowledge of how the customer interacts with and uses the service to realize new (or improved) value-creating processes.

An unused innovation is more or less worthless. Companies regard it as unused expense-only inventory item. It is also interesting to note that the original definition of innovation in the academic literature is based on whether or not the innovation is used in a market (making the

---

[1] Christensen, C.M., S.D. Anthony, G. Berstell, and D. Nitterhouse. 2007. "Finding the Right Job for Your Product." *MIT Sloan Management Review* 48, no. 3, pp. 38–49.

distinction to invention). This definition fits well with service logic and service innovation.

Service Innovation—A Changing Concept

Traditionally, innovations in the service sector have been regarded as a special type of technical innovation leading to the view of service innovation as something different or even odd. One reason is that it is regarded as different is that service innovations are seldom based on technical progress and patents (see Figure 2.2). They may encompass the process in which a company develops offerings containing aftermarket services, for example, repairs or maintenance of a certain type of machine, staff training, or financing. This has been done in the automotive industry by companies like Volvo, Caterpillar, and Scania. Service innovation has therefore been regarded as a so-called add-on, whose sole purpose is to maximize product performance without regard to the situation in which the customer operates. This outlook is based on viewing the product as the core component that creates value intrinsically. Services are launched to enable companies to improve the product further and thus make more money. One consequence of this outlook is the notion that it is a positive sign if a product is not working as it should, as the manufacturer will be able to sell more services (e.g., maintenance and repair). Companies that unwittingly work in this way will be faced with a very complicated relationship with quality and value. Furthermore, in developed countries, it is in reality the service part of the economy that is growing.

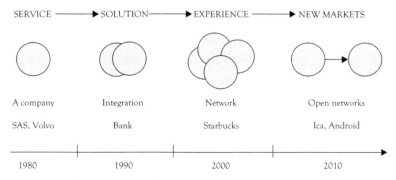

Figure 2.2 A perspective of service innovation

"Service with a smile" was a service innovation of the 1960s and 1970s as it became part of the script. The smiling service worker clearly enhanced the delivery experience in fast-food restaurants and hotel chains. Today flight attendants at Southwest Air have fun with customer recitations of safety warnings. In the 1990s, online banking was launched as a service to retail customers. Automated teller machines (ATMs) were a clear departure from friendly smiling personal bankers, but were fast, efficient, and available 24/7.

A step in the 1990s was the transition from developing service innovations within one single company to developing them by integrating resources of multiple companies. It led to companies offering complete solutions to the customers' problems as opposed to single services only. These solutions were created by combining different competencies or offerings into one solution. Instead of selling a product in the form of a machine and adding maintenance in the form of a service afterwards, companies started to offer solutions including maintenance of critical processes to the customer. These efforts facilitated the customer's value-creating process. Instead of, for instance, selling a saw to a customer, along with different types of associated maintenance services, the companies were now able to sell an offering consisting of taking responsibility for a certain amount of cutting lumber. Such an offer obviously included a machine (in this case a saw) and services; yet the unique aspects of this service innovation were based on the act of selling not only separate parts, but also the value-creating process the customer valued.

Servitization is discussed in the final chapter of this book, but it is worth noting here that "selling the job" is well established; IBM sells data processing power and computation time as an alternative to owning and managing a computer facility; IBM and Amazon offer businesses software and computing power in the cloud; GE sells hours of thrust, for example, "power by the hour," as an alternative to buying a jet engine (in truth this is an old concept from Rolls-Royce). Some roofers buy and then lease functioning roofs on business buildings! Pharmacies move in and take over inventories in hospitals to make sure that medication is not wasted and patient safety is not in danger. Although widespread, this approach is still far from universal.

Recently, there seems to be an increased focus on innovation of the service experience. In "The New Frontier of Experience Innovation" the authors call for service innovation that "allows individual customers to actively co-construct their own consumption experiences."[2] Brian Solis argues that "Customer experience is the new competitive advantage."[3]

In many traditional industries such as trade and catering, experiences were created via networks of companies that jointly generated value constellations for a particular experience. One example is Starbucks, which by viewing itself to be in the "experience business" has managed to change the practice of coffee drinking. This has been achieved via value networks covering the entire traditional value chain in which café employees address customers by their first name and deliver a good customer experience. For Starbucks, the brand and meaning of the brand becomes central in the value perception.

Using experiences as the goal of service innovation is not unique to the consumer industry—in the industrial sector, time management and increased competitiveness are important experiences resulting from service innovation. This process consists of generating value-creating processes by combining products and services, integrating them with the customer's business by, for instance, ensuring that they are adapted to the client company's employees, machines, and so on.

Some recent service innovation involves changing distribution channels or the nature of interaction with the customer. Services, along with tools for innovation, are offered on different platforms or arenas, such as Amazon or Android as well as other open markets. Android's case in particular involves providing open networks to enable other companies to develop and sell apps. This type of service innovation can offer a platform allowing other companies to either create service innovations directly or in collaboration with other actors. Service innovation by providing platforms for other companies' service innovations is of course not new and does not necessarily have to consist of information technology (IT), apps, or social media—for years, cooperative grocery distributors such as IGA in the United States and ICA in Sweden have allowed owners or retailers to adapt to their local market. This adoption could be to bring in unique

---

[2] Prahalad, C.K. and V. Ramaswamy. 2003. "The New Frontier of Experience Innovation." *Sloan Management Review* 44, no. 4, pp. 12–18.

[3] Solis, B. 2015. X: *The Experience When Business Meets Design*, 10. Hoboken, NJ: Wiley.

catering offerings or food (e.g., truffles, olive oil, or mozzarella cheese from regions in Italy) or create special events even outside the store.

These noted changes in innovation are consistent with a shift from product logic to service logic. Focus has shifted from products to how companies and organizations jointly create value with the customer. Moving from a perspective based on products to one based on facilitating value-creating processes represents a paradigm shift given the move away from the organization or company—an inward–outward paradigm—to viewing them as external parties reflecting on what resources may support the processes the customers are interested in achieving, an outward–inward paradigm.

The key components of a switch to an external focus on service innovation show that service innovation may come about in several different ways:

1. *Changing the role of the customer.* Give the customers a more active role! View customers as important resources in their own value-creating processes as opposed to passive recipients. Advice from staff and do-it-yourself (DIY) seminars are popular at stores such as Home Depot. Similarly, DIY videos are popular content on the websites of Advance Auto and other automobile supply retailers.

2. *Change processes.* Numerous companies have based value-creating processes on their own resources and opportunities to charge customers, but what happens when the customers' value-creating processes become the center of attention? For instance, instead of providing customers with a predetermined amount of one-size-fits-all or a limited number of packages of mobile services, smartphone customers can download whatever apps they need from a virtual market (the App Store) and in the process tailor the offering in accordance with their own needs.

3. *Fill an unsatisfied need.* Customers are good at stating their needs; however, all needs cannot be expressed. Some things are obviously difficult to describe—consider how hard it is to, for instance, describe how to dance or why it is so much fun. By the same token, customers might have unexpressed, latent, or emergent needs they are not

able to describe. As such, keep in mind that not all of the customers' needs can be expressed clearly and in simple terms. However, being able to meet needs—both explicit and implicit—will indeed result in very satisfied and loyal customers. Providing customizations tools, even as simple as Coke's mix-your-own-flavors vending machines, can tap into tacit or contextual needs.

4. *Break the value chain.* Are there new ways of providing value and concurrently increase the customer's options? Given the new service logic, the traditional value chains, in which products are refined in a multistage process, will soon be obsolete. An increasing number of companies are forming new value constellations to provide better value-creating processes. As an example, Ikea started collaborating with construction companies like Skanska and selling Whirlpool's kitchen appliances and TV sets or even apartments. All of this involves offering complete solutions to customers who would otherwise have been forced to spend a considerable amount of time matching kitchens with house layouts or TV sets with stereo furniture.

5. *New business models.* As noted, a number of companies are experimenting charging for the value-creating processes the customer actually experiences. A good example is GE's aircraft engines: Instead of charging for each individual aircraft engine, GE charges for the amount of time it is used or the thrust provided to the airline. The customer's value-creating processes do not begin until the aircraft is used. The customer's experience, which is a product of the value-creating processes, will result in GE being regarded as an important partner that helps them achieve the desired results. It is likely that there will be a greater focus on the service components of the business.

6. *Study customer processes.* Customers sometimes come up with their own solutions to a problem, by modifying an existing service or good or by creating their own. This often happens when none of the existing services on the market is adequate to advance the customer's value-creating processes. In the 1970s, Professor Eric von Hippel identified a "customer active paradigm" of innovation where driven customers, even in B2B markets, made modifications to existing

offerings.[4] When the Tribune Company launched the *RedEye* tabloid it planned for a rapid change in response to user feedback: daily reader interviews and surveys fed into overnight changes in layout. Within a week the tabloid was significantly changed; in two months, it was a dramatically different publication. Game companies and software companies invite users to post customizations to their company websites. Service innovation is enhanced by observing, embracing, and facilitating customer innovation.

Radical, Incremental, and Recombinative Service Innovation

A traditional service innovation perspective is based on the notion that innovation takes place via changes in service attributes. Said service attributes are, in turn, represented by the provider's attributes, the customer's attributes, and the offering's attributes. Such a change can be radical, incremental, or take place by combining different kinds of offerings or attributes. The latter is actually one of the most frequent forms of service innovation.

Innovation by changing the customer's attributes can be illustrated by Millstores, a U.S. retailer that offers unfinished wood furniture that customers can finish or paint to their wishes and the Swedish home-improvement chain Byggmax, where customers themselves select and cut the lumber they wish to buy. The service prerequisites in this case are based on activities carried out by the customers themselves (in this case, the new service consists of a more affordable offer to the customer and the experience of participation more actively in the solution).

Finally, innovation can also occur by changing attributes of the offering, as illustrated by the coffee company Löfbergs. The value is not only derived from enjoying a warm cup of coffee—it is just as much a social lubricant. Value can be extracted from the fact that the coffee may have been harvested in a fair and ecological way. Perhaps, you can feel that you are a better or more concerned person than someone who buys his or her

---

[4] von Hippel, E. 1978. "Successful Industrial Products from Customer Ideas." *The Journal of Marketing* 42, no. 1, pp. 39–49.

coffee from a standard coffee shop. For Löfbergs the coffee is what is key and for them it is important that you buy the right coffee based on your own taste. Consequently, they arrange coffee tasting and allow you to pick beans and roasting that are right for you.

A radical innovation involves extensive underlying change in attributes. The entire service system is often modified, leading to profound changes in most or all service attributes. The tabloid newspapers *Metro* and *RedEye*, which were described in Chapter 1, are considered examples of a radical innovation since they brought about a change in the entire traditional newspaper distribution and financing system. (The *Metro* and *RedEye* tabloid newspapers may also be considered "disruptive innovations," as they meet the Christensen criteria of originating as cheaper and lower quality competitors overlooked by established participants.[5])

An incremental innovation only entails minor changes in the service system. Ironically, a company may have to engage in a series of incremental innovations to facilitate absorption of radical changes by customers. Incremental innovation is often an efficiency improvement from both the customer's and the company's points of view. For example, to facilitate the flow of customers, Ikea is currently redesigning the outline and navigation of its stores to mimic the design of airports. By this means that it should be easier to find a faster way through the store.

Most innovations are "recombinative" innovation that consists of the development of a service by combining one or more existing offerings or solutions or changing the current combination of offerings in the service. Recombinative innovation consists of changes in the underlying technique or a bundling of existing solutions. They can also be created by unbundling an existing solution into several different ones. Recombinative innovation may be the most common type of service innovation. The process is based on companies merging an established solution with either a completely new one or one that has been part of a previous offering.

A newspaper subscription containing both a printed copy and an electronic version is an example of recombinative innovation. Travel magazines have existed for a long time as a separate offering, this can also be

---

[5] Christensen, C.M. 2003. *The Innovator's Dilemma: The Revolutionary Book that Will Change the Way You Do Business*, 320. New York: HarperBusiness Essentials.

added to the newspaper which again is a recombination. Swedish Linas matkasse (Lina's grocery bag) is another exciting example. For a long time, trials were carried out in which grocery bags were customized and delivered to customers after they had placed their orders. This concept suffered from problems in the form of expensive and complicated logistics. By streamlining orders so that grocery bags contained the same kind of items, planning routes for each delivery, and combining the delivery of food with recipes, Linas matkasse was able to create a successful service innovation. Again, this is in essence not really new if we look at the separate components, what is unique is the combination.

A New Model of Service Innovation

Service innovation should be based on the needs of customers and their value-creating processes. It is therefore rare that service innovations encompass only part of a company's or organization's business—rather, they involve many different components, often the customers themselves, especially in the case of radical service innovation. Instead of the traditional approach we have chosen to divide service innovation into six categories based on the purpose they are designated to fulfill (see Figure 2.4):

- Process innovation
- Business model innovation
- Brand innovation
- Experience innovation
- Social innovation
- Behavioral innovation

We should point out the potential for overlap between different categories—a process innovation can, for instance, be combined with a business model innovation. However, all innovations do have a starting point; where a company wants to have an impact with their innovation. The main focus could be to target a more efficient process (process innovation) and this may affect the brand. We hope this categorization of service innovation makes the planning and execution of new service development projects easier.

Let us begin with the axes that are illustrated in Figure 2.3. One often requested value-creating process is reducing the costs of offerings. This causes many service innovations to revolve around streamlining the process and several such examples have already been mentioned. Retailers such as Home Depot and Advance Auto for instance serve the DIY segment, allowing customers to save money. The term lean is closely related to what companies want to accomplish in this category and do remember that lean can be a term for both production and consumption.

Another important value-creating process is differentiation, which is represented by the other end of the horizontal axis in Figure 2.3. Differentiation refers to a new kind of service (based on a number of resources) with distinguishing characteristics. If a company combines enough characteristics it makes the offering difficult to copy. Starbucks is an example here; in essence, Starbucks is another coffee shop but it does have a number of innovations that make it unique. They have their own beans, they sell music, their delivery process entails learning your first name, the constantly renew their offerings. Another coffee company may copy one of the characteristics but the complete offering is difficult to mimic.

In Figure 2.3, streamline and differentiate are represented as two end points of a continuum, which, with an additional axis representing

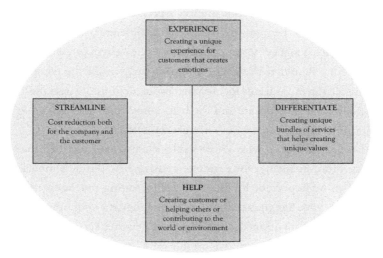

Figure 2.3 Two axes to understand different types of service innovation

"experience" and "help," aid us to define six different types of service innovations in Figure 2.4. The value-creating process, experience, addresses the customers' need to be exposed to different kinds of unique experiences. Such experiences result in emotions and most examples in the research literature, relate to traveling (e.g., rafting), music concerts, or spa treatments. Experiences, could just as well relate to feelings occurring after a desirable outcome, for example, when medicine starts to work and symptoms are relieved, or in B2B contexts when customers contact a company after seeing their latest marketing campaign. The creation of the Apple stores is another good example where the experience was a central component.

On the opposite side of the axis, we find the value-creating process, help. This encompasses community involvement where customers simply want to contribute to the well-being of other people or to the world or environment. There are numerous examples of this increasingly popular type of social innovation—the company RelayRides allows you to rent a neighbor's car, thereby saving money on a car rental and contributing to reduced resource use; Tom's Shoes donates shoes to poor children for every purchase; and a Swedish company with the clever name Bee Urban rents out beehives to companies and thereby contributes to a more ecological and sustainable society.

Another interesting feature of these aspects is how easy it is to replicate the innovations. The innovations targeted at differentiation or experience are generally designed to be difficult to replicate by competitors; these innovations should truly set the company apart from the competitors. This while the innovations focused on cost reductions or streamlining are generally easier to replicate and the help innovations are something that is meant to be replicated by other organizations.

Let us now look at what is covered by the two axes and their four end points. Since financing, for example, creating new business models, has proved to be important for the four value-creating processes just mentioned, we have designated financing as the model's midpoint. Also, the other examples mentioned, in the form of new markets, fit this type of service innovation. As such, we do not only have four extremes on two axes, but also a midpoint in our service innovation business model. We

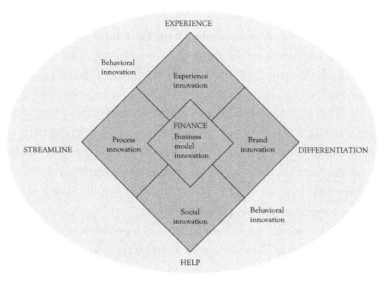

Figure 2.4 Six categories of service innovation

have placed the other six innovation categories around this midpoint. The basic value-creating processes we have described earlier—the two axes in Figure 2.3—are summarized in Figure 2.4.

Process innovations refer to service innovations that provide a higher efficiency or assistance to the customer. An example of a process innovation is a self-service feature, having customers do part of the work themselves. Self-service may create value by lowering cost, saving time, increasing hours of availability, or even increasing customer satisfaction. If customers fetch goods at the warehouse and solve various problems via the Internet, technical devices, or open warehouses, staff will be freed to carry out other tasks in the company. This also makes the customers feel that the value they are interested can be achieved in a more efficient manner—they do not need to conform to specific times, wait in line, and then explain their errand to an employee. The down side is that by not meeting employees the customers get distanced from the company and do not build relationships in the same way making a firm easier to be replaced by a competitor.

Research also shows that there are segments of customers who appreciate not having to interact with employees and who choose self-service if offered.[6] Self-service in large supermarkets has become a popular and appreciated feature. At Ikea, customers get products themselves at the warehouse, transport it home themselves, and assemble them when they get home. Tasks carried out by a carpenter in the traditional value chain are now carried out by the consumer, leading to a collective cost-saving benefit. The customers' own efforts do not only save time and money but may also make it easier for them to reach key goals. Just to emphasize the ease of coping for streamlining, one of Ikea's main innovation has been the flat packages for their furnitures. Instead of transporting air Ikea can optimize their logistics and really pack their trucks full. Now look what all other companies are doing in this industry.

In health care, the patients' own efforts are a prerequisite for successful treatment of certain illnesses. Home monitoring may become as common as having consumers brush their own teeth for dental hygiene. In a health care project involving several of the authors, researchers found that the treatment time for a particular type of illness could be shortened to five days if radiological examinations, diagnosis, and surgery were carried out when it fitted the patient instead of fitting with the organization. In current practice, it took 105 days for the patient to reach the last treatment stage. Shifting the focus to the patients' perspective could help us to design a process innovation with benefits for both the patient and society. Another example of streamlining with a focus on lean.

Brand innovation aims to find ways to differentiate offerings from those of competitors. The goal is to form a new bundle of solutions (think bundle of services) that improves value to customers who thereby perceive the offering as particularly important. The brand and what it is related to can be an important part of the product experience; so brand innovation can facilitate value creation. In order to succeed in brand innovation, companies need to take into account the basic service offering, the strategy and direction it is aiming for, and what the new service is supposed to create. For example, an affordable travel solution would bundle low-cost

---

[6] Meuter, M.L., A.L. Ostrom, M.J. Bitner, and R. Roundtree. 2003. "The Influence of Technology Anxiety on Consumer Use and Experiences with Self-Service Technologies." *Journal of Business Research* 56, no. 11, pp. 899–906.

airplane seats with affordable accommodation offerings—not a selection of five-star hotels.

To succeed in brand innovation, the service innovation also needs to fit in with the existing company or organization. It would likely be detrimental for Tag Heuer or Rolex to start selling their watches more cheaply on the Internet. Understanding customers, how they view the brand, and how a brand innovation would affect their use and experience of a service, is a prerequisite for success.

In our research we have measured how long it will take to assimilate and start using new solutions, which we refer to as technology readiness among organizations and customers. The technology readiness of older customers (or patients) of health care and social organizations is generally below average. The health and social care organizations we have encountered have to build a brand of personal services and meetings. Trying to develop value-creating processes aimed at efficiency or self-service IT solutions would not help the customers (patients) at all, even if it saved the existing organization money in the short term. However, for certain types of patients self-service IT solutions can aid in value creation, and then freed resources can be used for other patients.

All service innovations are based on experiences; so feelings arise when value is created. A patient who has been relieved of elbow pain via physiotherapy probably experiences feelings of relief and joy. Sometimes the emotional impact of the experience is the focus of a service. Recall the examples of experience innovation from Chapter 1 including wildlife adventures or hiring a star chef.

Another variant of experience innovation focuses on the "servicescape," where experience landscapes are represented by a store, restaurant, theme park, or some other location in which customers may interact with staff. The purpose of such changes is not only to augment the customers' brand experience but also to encourage a different type of behavior. Experiments in servicescape have been carried out in Swedish retailer Telia's stores where some of the employees have acted as hosts rather than salespersons with the purpose of letting customers experience Telia as a company that takes care of its customers as opposed to focusing solely on sales. The results of adding a host-like salesperson show that with a host the customers' feels like that have waited less time and that they explore the store more. Abercrombie & Fitch is famous for its novel in-store experiences offered to customers, with live models in the entrance or transition zone into their stores. Ikea created stores entire families go to without any prior plans of buying anything. A trip to Ikea can be regarded as a viable alternative to a café visit or a day at the zoo and therefore represents a true experience innovation. Disney has worked to create a positive experience in the lines waiting to ride attractions in its theme parks, that is, turning waiting time into play time.

Some service innovations aim to contribute to a better world. This is usually referred to as social innovation and encompasses innovative ideas aimed at improving something missing or not working in society. Microlenders or microcredits firms such as Opportunity International or Grameen Bank fight poverty through small loans to very small businesses, often owned by women. Another example is Khan Academy, which actively works with increasing children's and young people's knowledge and interest in mathematics, science, and other key subjects. Free self-paced online educational services and instruction are available to students in grades K–12.

Social innovations can originate with individuals. "Paused coffee" at a café involves buying an extra cup that "rests" until someone, unknown to the benefactor, shows up and wants a cup of coffee but cannot afford it. As December 25 approaches, some Walmart and Kmart customers, referred to as "layaway angels," pay the remaining amount outstanding on children's gifts being held for strangers in the layaway section, in order to make sure that the children will have gifts to open on Christmas day. In Norway, some landowners have developed a practice called Epleslang, where people with apple trees allow others to "steal" apples from them. The apples are then handed in to stores that press apple juice from them and donate the revenue to those in need. City Harvest (New York) and similar "food rescue" organizations throughout the world collect food that would otherwise be thrown away and distribute it to those in need. The underlying assumption of these service innovations is that they should be easy to replicate rather than a money making machine.

Business model innovation is a diverse category in which innovations are often formed via multiple categories of service innovation. The key event in business model innovation is a change in the manner (model) a company makes its money, leading to improved value-creating processes for the customer. The organization's external or internal environment changes in such a way that revenue streams can be redirected to enable win–win situations for several parties. One example already mentioned is the tabloid newspapers *RedEye* (Chicago) and *Metro* (Sweden). By changing the distribution system and pricing, customers could read a newspaper for free (business model, cost saving, and efficiency), while the organization benefited from increased advertising revenue. Aside from a clever search algorithm, Google's search engine owes its success to the value network built around the service. The customer does not pay for the service—advertisers instead pay Google to show advertisements to the customer. Google then employed that same free-service-with-advertising model to make Android a dominant smartphone platform.

A number of business model innovations let customers pay on a per-use basis for a service instead of buying physical products. One example of this is the bicycles you as a visitor can rent in different cities around the world, you just check them out using your credit card and return them at your leasure. Such business models are appealing because the customer's payment is directly connected to its value-creating processes. Another example is building a platform that facilitates customer meetings and subsequently charging for business activities that take place on it. The most successful and interesting business models are often based on charging for results (i.e., value-creating process) of what is offered. For instance, increasing customer productivity would make it advantageous to charge for the increase in productivity rather than charging for the amount of time spent carrying out the work that induced the increase.

As soon as actors in a market launch new business models, other (competing) organizations are often forced to follow. One example is the change currently taking place in traditional manufacturing industries, where companies are increasingly shifting their focus away from making money on the product to generating increasingly higher revenue from services. Since the service is often more closely connected to the value-creating process, common business acumen suggests that it is more beneficial to make money on the service rather than on the product. The product then becomes a platform for the service, which enables a new business model for the customer and increased revenue for the provider. Noted companies such as IBM, Volvo, GE Aircraft, and Ericsson are attempting to increase the sales of services through offerings.

The last category of service innovation is behavioral innovation, which focuses on bringing about a change in the customer's behavior. All service innovations involve change in customer behavior since the customer always plays an active part in the value creation, but we feel that this category is important and interesting enough to be highlighted in its own right (which it is why it is displayed at the bottom or as the platform of Figure 2.4). One example of behavior innovation occurs when companies and public organizations want to help customers change their behavior for the public good. For instance, what could encourage us to ride the bus more often, use less energy during peak hours, eat more ecological food, or make decisions that benefit our environment or our own health? Some energy utilities have found it helpful to let homeowners know if they seem to be using more energy than their neighbors—people seem to want to be as green as their neighbors. The health care industry focuses on getting patients to take prescribed medicine in a safe manner and both the health and fitness industries focus on getting people to exercise.

There are numerous behavior innovations that do not originate from organizations but from customers who begin to use products or services in an unintended way. One striking example is the explosion of short messaging service (SMS) traffic beginning in 1999 that led to a radical change in behavior (in a way that surprised telecommunication operators). Another example of behavior innovation can be found in social media, where users in a large number of areas share clever applications, as well as ways of using offerings that companies probably would not have thought of. A new social network, Slack, was designed for internal business use but is being used by individuals as another social network for groups. Such use spreads fast and can be quickly organized via blogs.

Table 2.1 illustrates the six innovation categories. One might ask whether we have been able to cover all types of service innovations in this model. The answer is hopefully (!), "no," since creative and entrepreneurial companies and organizations come up with new ways of developing their ability to facilitate value-creating processes for customers. New innovations will undoubtedly appear over time and the categories we have used may then prove to be incapable of describing the process at hand. However, overall value creating goals, such as streamline, differentiate, experience, and help, will always be important to the customer.

Table 2.1 Different categories of service innovation

Category	Explanation or a streamlining
Process innovation	An efficiency-improving service innovation on the customer's part. One example could be a self-service that makes it easier for the customer to create value.
Brand innovation	A service innovation that differentiates the offering to the customer, thereby creating value. One example could be expensive watches that add free cleaning and maintenance once a year.
Experience innovation	All service innovations lead to experiences. However, service innovation often refers to a service that facilitates new experiences for the customer. One possible example could be a new type of holidays or hotels.
Social innovation	A service innovation that quite simply contributes to a better world. This could be innovations that help people that need help, like distributing food or get people in work that are far from the job market.
Business model innovation	The service innovation that leads to a change in how the service provider makes money. When this change occurs, positive value-creating processes are created even for the customer. Charging for news articles on the Internet, which is a standard procedure for a lot of newspapers, is one example of a modified business model in the media industry.
Behavior innovation	A service innovation that leads to a change in customer behavior. In essence, all service innovations involve changing customer behavior, although some lead to greater changes than others. The introduction of smartphones paved the way for an entire array of new behavior innovations.

A Note on Collaborative Economy

One phenomenon connected to service innovation that seems to be booming at the moment is the collaborative economy or sharing economy. A definition of collaborative economy is to use a platform connected to the Internet in order to efficiently match people's wants with people's haves. We all have our favorite examples of this, such as Airbnb, which enables people to rent out their homes or unused spare rooms, or Uber that connects people in need of a ride with people who have a car. The list of examples of areas that the collaborative ideas are applied to can be made very long, for example, Peer-to-Peer Lending, Crowdfunding, Apartment or House Renting, Ridesharing and Carsharing, Coworking, Reselling and Trading, Knowledge and Talent-Sharing, and Niche Services. The systems can be seen to innovate different types of market behaviors such as renting, lending, swapping, sharing, bartering, and gifting in new ways and at a scale that was not possible before the Internet.

Summary and Additional Reading

This chapter covered categories of service innovation. Service logic dictates that everything can be regarded as a service in the sense that it is a perspective on value creation. It is important to think in these terms and understand what your company actually provides. Substantial efforts are required before such a philosophy can be applied in practice. Service innovation logic is different from new product development.

We focus on the goals of service innovation. We associate brand innovation with differentiate, business model innovation with finance, process innovation with streamline, experience innovation with positive experiences, social innovation with helping, and behavior innovation with behavioral change. There is, of course, a certain degree of overlap between the different types of service innovations, but an overall focus helps point out a general direction that might lead to the fulfillment of other purposes. Financing or the business model, for instance, is a component found in all other innovations: How would you make money on your next innovation in a smart way that also is beneficial for the customer and potential partners?

Action questions for the service innovator:

- What other products and services do your customers use with your offerings to do their "job" or create value?
- What knowledge and activities are required in order for the customer to create value with a proposed service innovation?
- Is there a way to make it easier for the customers to combine needed services and knowledge to do the "job" they want done? Has someone attempted to make such coordination possible? Are you working on such a solution?

- Review recent service innovations in *your* organization. Which service innovation categories (see Figure 2.3 or Table 2.1) have been undertaken? Which categories have seemed more successful for your organization? Which categories have been neglected?
- Can you envision a business model innovation in the market your organization serves?

The main sources of inspiration for this chapter are:

Gallouj, F., and O. Weinstein. 1997. "Innovation in Services." *Research Policy* 26, no. 4, pp. 537–56.

Michel, S., S.W. Brown, and A.S. Gallan. 2008. "Service-Logic Innovations: How to Innovate Customers, Not Products." *California Management Review* 50, no. 3, pp. 49–65.

Sawhney, M., S. Balasubramanian, and V.V. Krishnan. 2003. "Creating Growth with Services." MIT Sloan Management Review 45, no. 2, pp. 34–44.

Ulwick, A. 2005. *What Customers Want: Using Outcome-Driven Innovation to Find High-Growth Opportunities, Create Breakthrough Products and Services.* New York: McGraw-Hill.

CHAPTER 3

Value Creation Drives Service Innovation

Remember, in the future, the brand is owned by the consumer, not by the company.

—Martin Lindström

We are what we repeatedly do. Excellence then, is not a single act, but a habit.

—Aristotle

This chapter focuses on the importance of understanding "value in use"— the value-creation process of the customer's. Questionnaires, focus groups, and even in-depth interviews rely on a customer's memory of this process. Research shows, however, that people are not very good at remembering such activities in detail. Organizations must therefore utilize user research methods that uncover needs and be customer-oriented in order to meet those needs.

Preview of Action Questions

Action questions for the innovator reading this chapter include:

- Who in your organization observes users creating value with your services?
- How is user knowledge (1) saved and (2) put to work?
- Is your organization truly customer oriented?

Understanding the Customer's Value-Creation Processes

As discussed in the previous chapters, value is created through the use of products or services. The process can be very context or situation specific. For most coffee drinkers, the value of coffee is greater in the morning than at night and the first cup of the day is the most valuable. In order to understand the real value to a customer, it is necessary to understand how, why, and in what context a service is used. A service can be perceived incorrectly if we fail to take into account the context.

Comparing the development of digital cameras with built-in cameras in mobile phones helps us understand how the perception of value is dependent on context. Advanced system cameras still take significantly better pictures than a mobile phone. However, mobile phone cameras provide acceptable quality *and* are at hand for photo-worthy moments, while a camera is too often lying at home in a drawer. The golden moments, such as a child taking its first steps, are thus more likely to be captured on a mobile phone. Cameras have enjoyed spectacular technical development, but since their use is limited to photography and requires planning and configuration, they are often not at hand when a moment worth photographing occurs. Thus, nonprofessional photographers take more, and more valuable, photos with mobile phone cameras than they do with technically advanced digital system cameras.

Once again, an exclusive focus on the product or technical solution is insufficient. Offering a fabulous direct or indirect service is not enough—companies must also understand the full context of the customers' value-creation processes. The study of fast-food milk shakes discussed in Chapter 2 illustrates the importance of context. A relatively simply product was used for very different purposes in the morning and in the evening. In the morning, commuters used milk shakes to make a boring commute more interesting and pleasurable; in the evening, parents used them to reward or bribe their children. The difference in value creation or jobs performed by the simple product led to the conclusion that thicker milk shakes would enhance the experience of morning users, while thinner ones would improve value creation in the evening!

The interaction between the customer and company during customer value creation is important. For instance, when a bank clerk gives advice, the value of the advice is not only based on the customer's financial situation, but also on how well the customer is able to answer questions and, in turn, how adept the clerk is at understanding the customer's situation and asking the right questions. The customer and the bank interact jointly to create value for the customer. The customer's situation and interaction with the service supplier have proven very difficult to understand.

It is difficult to guess in advance what kind of value-creating processes the customer prefers. In addition, the value of the customer's own efforts (the interaction) is too often forgotten by the company. The customer should not be viewed as a passive participant—someone who is served. Let us use an example from the electronics industry by analyzing a company advertisement (see Figure 3.1).

The product details of the TV in Figure 3.1 give the impression that the components' technical specifications are solely responsible for the value-creating process. Value is generated by the TV and the customer only needs to passively view it. The technical solutions found in the advertisement—described in the form of abbreviations and trademarked terms—are apportioned a large amount of space, and, as a consequence, very few words are dedicated to explaining the experiences a customer is expected to enjoy by using this particular TV. How "S Recommendation" is valuable to the customer is uncertain. "Sell the benefits, not the features"

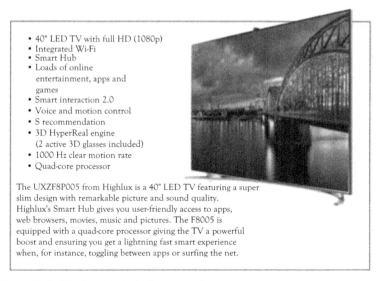

Figure 3.1 Product details from an electronics store

is a well-known sales slogan, but some firms still talk about technical specifications and believe they will do the job without considering the cocreation of the customer. Service innovators might update the slogan to "Sell the value, not the features."

Fancy acronyms or technical jargon do not generate value. If the customer wishes to increase family bonds by watching TV in the living room, the choice of TV program may have a significantly greater impact than the technical attributes of the TV. The customer's ability to use the features, for instance, by connecting the TV to other devices, impacts value creation. A 40-in. TV may appear diminutive in a very large room, but could be too big for a small student flat. The context and interaction determine the value and the technical features are just tools that might influence value creation.

Value-Creating Processes Are Difficult to Capture

Research literature often describes customers' value-creating processes as hard to capture or "sticky." In addition to being context specific and subjective, the information is only interpretable and understandable by the person experiencing the value, making it difficult to transfer, hence being "sticky." The fact that information is difficult to interpret without the customer stresses the importance of including customers or users in the development process. Stickiness can be rooted in the fact that the information is largely based on what users take for granted; consequently, there is no guarantee that users will be able to recall said information in a survey, focus group, or an in-depth interview. User research is often conducted in an antithetical context (often at a company) and point in time compared to the real context in which value is created. A successful interview depends on asking the interviewees perceptive questions that encompass the value experienced by a customer and the customer's ability to provide rich, detailed answers. The answers must then be interpreted by the interviewer or a research team in such a way that they can be transformed into information useful to the company at a later stage.

Interview methodology and concomitant focus groups are based on a passive view of customers. If a service offering is totally new, usage is difficult to imagine—possibly unthinkable in advance. Customers can only respond to what they have experienced, for example, existing services. Too often user research seems to assume that as long as the customers are asked the right questions, they will give the "right answer."

A more active view of customers regards them as coproducers or cocreators of value. Their more active role generates more understanding and ideas than from answering predefined (and often incorrectly posed) questions. A contributing factor to why new company offerings some-times fail is that companies have more knowledge of their own offerings than of the customers' needs for the solution contained in the service or product. This might result in a new technical solution, as in Table 3.1, built on technology that the customer does not understand and perhaps has no use of. Companies and organizations do indeed have employees with great solution development skills; yet very few know how to analyze and appreciate the customers' needs.

Our studies show that companies should continue to communicate with customers during the development process in order to understand how a solution may be used to meet the customers' needs, as knowledge of their situations and interactions is best acquired through long-term communication.

The aforementioned context gives rise to the concept market-driven service innovation or outside-in perspective, which is based on a deeper understanding of the customers' cocreative efforts and contexts. The innovations also utilize the fact that many customers appreciate being actively involved in contributing to a service or physical product so that it better matches their needs. For clarity we want to stress that this does not exclusively involve explicit needs, but also implicit and perhaps even as-yet undiscovered, so-called latent, needs. The latter can be difficult to articulate and predict. The methods for discovering and verifying those types of needs often involve staying close to customer markets, interactions, or communications. The customers' value-creating processes are not best analyzed in a clinical office environment—rather, the company must be proactive and interact with customers in the environment where they actually use the services. In addition to immersing themselves in customer information, companies essentially need methods that follow the customers in their own context—or location—in order to understand how they think.

We contrast market-driven service innovations to innovation that stems from a "laboratory" or internal development process. We want to emphasize the importance that company staff personally get to know their customers and contexts via personal experiences, and to only use intermediary actors as complementary tools. We will also illustrate how a company should try to involve customers in development processes in order to gain access to their experience and competence. We also want to stress that this curiosity about the customer has to be built into a company's culture—a company needs to realize that customers do have good ideas.

Customers Have Good Ideas!

Innovation is all about matching a solution to a need. Historically, those in possession of the solutions are companies that are supposed to chase information about user needs. However, there are numerous examples of customers finding good solutions to problems or needs themselves. Many of the products we use on a daily basis originate from customer ideas—everything from chips, coffee filters, and chocolate chip cookies to Frisbees, rollerblades, and computer operating systems. Our research has shown that, given the right circumstances, customers are capable of developing ideas that are both more creative and of higher user value than ideas originating from company product developers.[1] This is not that strange since users are more aware of their own needs and often have ideas on how to meet them. The challenge for a company to involve customers as developers is to provide the customers with the tools needed to successfully innovate service.

Companies often use highly educated engineers, expert in the underlying technology, to find new solutions and products. This can be a source of development problems. Consider a service solution designed for teenagers. Most company developers would have a completely different set of values, behavioral patterns, income sources, and priorities

---

[1] Kristensson, P., A. Gustafsson, and T. Archer. 2004. "Harnessing the Creative Potential Among Users." *Journal of Product Innovation Management* 21, no. 1, pp. 4–14.

than teenagers, making it very difficult to understand what the target customers want and are willing to pay for. This could be an excellent opportunity for the target group—the teenagers—to become innovators as they possess the knowledge of elusive (hard-to-capture) needs, namely their own experiences and value-creating processes.

An additional reason why customers are sometimes better equipped for creative success in innovation than companies is their less restricted thought patterns. Customers are simply not aware of how the current solution works, the limits on the current technology used, what has been the company tradition, or how the competition might respond, making it easier to think freely.

Take text messages (short messaging service or "SMS") as an example—the Finnish engineer Matti Makkonen has described how he and two of his colleagues brainstormed the SMS into existence over a few beers and a pizza in 1984.[2] It took 10 years, however, until the first text message was sent, and even then, no one imagined it would amount to anything more than a way for businessmen trying to reach each other in the absence of other forms of communication! Makkonen et al. thought that they had invented a service exclusively for businessmen.

The operators hesitated to charge for sending an SMS since they judged the market to be small but the newly developed service could be a good differentiator for the operator. The rest is history, as individual users became the services' most fervent users. Texting was an excellent source of income for mobile operators for many years. SMS was not the result of a meticulously planned process; it illustrates the difficulty involved in predicting innovation success. Customers need to be involved from the start of an innovation process to enable an understanding of value-generating processes.

It is not always easy for the customers to provide comprehensive information on how they act, think, or live. "Sticky" information is so obvious to customers and users that they cannot correctly describe it from memory without forgetting important details. Think of how you would give directions to your home—you would probably forget some important

---

[2] http://www.dailymail.co.uk/news/article-3147148/He-gr8-man-Inventor-text-message-Matti-Makkonen-dies-aged-63.html

details because you would most likely take it for granted. Alternatively, try explaining to a teenager how they should think and act when driving a car—it is extremely difficult! The reason for this is that we establish automated routines or mental shortcuts in our brains (heuristics). If this process of automation never took place, every routine activity would be far too resource intensive for our brains, which would not be sustainable in the long term. However, the use of mental shortcuts also makes it more difficult to explain our routine actions to any external party. It is also expensive and time consuming for companies to acquire and understand this type of information. Therefore it may be best to involve the customers in the development of new service directly.

Research results generally show that companies are not adept at using the customer to improve or create innovative solutions for their products. Many companies understand the benefit of using customer information, and are even willing to open up the organization and invite the customer in; yet very few are skilled at really utilizing customer information during the development of new services. The culprit is, again, routine behavior—not having performed a procedure previously makes it difficult to implement constructively on a bigger scale.

In our estimation, most companies have a bias to solutions developed internally. Many have a proud and strong tradition of implementing inward–outward innovations, preferably in laboratory settings, which leads to a potential lack of aptitude for listening to, or analyzing, customers and their value-creating processes. Companies are often solution oriented and possess a profound technical understanding. These companies' main weakness lies in the choice of working according to an outward–inward paradigm. Our research studies indicate that companies rely excessively on consultants for understanding users, and organizational knowledge of how to gather customer knowledge is often lacking. This is unacceptable: Companies have to acquire their own competence and understand their customers; customer understanding must be considered a core competency. Yet, several studies show that even when companies conduct customer surveys, interviews, or focus groups, the results are not necessarily ever used or distributed within the organizations.

The Right Method at the Right Time

Our research uncovers a pervasive lack of company knowledge of the applicability of user research methods in service innovation development.[3] Many companies are not aware of the strengths and weaknesses of different market research tools. Consider a toolbox: In the same way hammers and screwdrivers are useful for a certain set of tasks and useless for others, focus groups or ethnographical studies are useful for certain types of information acquisition. Table 3.1 contains a classification of some of the most common research tools available. Please note that Table 3.1 is not a comprehensive list of research methods but an overview.

As shown in Table 3.1, the prevailing customer information strategy in companies is based on using information stored internally in the organization. This information may consist of customer complaints, warranty claims for previous products, or information from salespersons. Using only this type of information in the development process may lead to minor improvements of existing products, but may also lead an organization to miss key opportunities. In addition, customer information is reformulated and reinterpreted—from salespersons to marketers to developers—in a multistage process that will likely simplify or distort it. Moreover, this specific type of information is not centrally compiled for use during development. Table 3.1 indicates that this type of information is appropriate when the company is improving existing services and that it may also be regarded as a gold mine for preventive actions. In particular, it is possible to find problems that have previously been overlooked or minimized.

Customer surveys are often carried out with traditional methods such as in-depth interviews, focus groups and surveys, and often marketed as miracle tools capable of revealing every possible customer secret. Focus groups and questionnaires, in particular,

---

[3] Witell, L., P. Kristensson, A. Gustafsson, and M. Löfgren. 2011. "Idea Generation: Customer Co-Creation Versus Traditional Market Research Techniques." *Journal of Service Management* 22, no. 2, pp. 140–59.

Table 3.1 Research methods used in a service innovation process

	Service improvement	Incremental service innovations	Radical service innovations
Focus	Reactive	Reactive	Proactive
Methods	Complaints Critical events Observations	Focus groups In-depth interviews Questionnaires	Lead user methods Customer involvement Ethnographical studies
Comments	This method category is based on existing information or information on typical problems experienced by the customer	This method category is based on how companies should consolidate their existing strengths and involves what customers have experiences after the fact	This method category captures information in the customers' own context and is based on their actions, often in real time

have enjoyed considerable popularity. Focus groups are based on gathering at least six customers (not more than 12) to carrying out structured group discussions in a particular area of focus. However, focus groups may be useful if wanting to acquire large amounts of data at a relatively low cost. Another advantage is that it taps into the human ability to stimulate interparty discussions. The negative aspect though is the relatively small amount of discussion time allotted to each individual and that the discussion can easily be taken over by anyone with strong views. Imagine a focus group of eight people. The average group will convene for approximately two hours. Evenly distributing the discussion time leaves 15 minutes per person. Since every person's contribution to the discussion will be fragmented, it is quite obvious that this method will not paint a particularly clear picture of an individual customer.

Furthermore, group dynamics limit the creativity and quality of new service ideas generated through group brainstorming and focus groups. A recent review of 50 years of empirical evidence on generating ideas from these group methods shows that individual interviews or even individual brainstorming produce (1) more ideas for innovation, (2) higher quality ideas, and (3) more radical ideas than group methods, even when the total time per participant is equal.[4]

In-depth interviews have the advantage of providing a more complete picture of the customers' views, but time consumption and difficulty carrying them out practically are obvious disadvantages. In-depth interviews and focus groups too rarely take place in the customer's own locale or context and customers are instead expected to recall information during the interview. Questionnaires are used to test new hypotheses, but only reflect information contained in questions compiled by the interviewer beforehand. What is never asked will never be answered, and there is a risk the questioner is not aware of areas relevant to the customer's value creation.

The aforementioned methods may be categorized as reactive and are suitable when customers are supposed to react to what already exists, that is, a service the customers have experienced or a situation they have found themselves in with some degree of continuity. The customers answer the questions based on what they recall or think they recall from past experiences. Some things are, however, unimaginable in advance and it is very difficult to react to something that has not been previously experienced; hence, many customers often resort to their best guess. Many are the companies that have acted on information that indicate a need for a particular solution, only to have the customers turn their backs on them after developing and offering what they purportedly wanted!

A chapter on user research for product innovation in the *PDMA Handbook of New Product Development* cited sticky information in the story of a small team developing the first Internet-based system for settlement of exchange traded derivatives held by financial institutions.[5]

---

[4] Schirr, G.R. 2012. "Flawed Tools: The Efficacy of Group Research Methods to Generate Customer Ideas." *Journal of Product Innovation Management* 29, no. 3, pp. 473–88.

[5] Schirr, G.R. 2012. "User Research for Product Innovation." In *The PDMA Handbook of New Product Development*, eds. K.B. Kahn, S.E. Kay, R.J. Slotegraaf, and S. Uban. Hoboken, NJ: John Wiley & Sons, Inc. doi:10.1002/9781118466421.ch14

A client referred to as "Alice" had been extremely cooperative with the development team. She had shared her frustrations with her current vendor, who was the market leader, and had given the team a detailed view of how that competitor's service worked.

One day Alice and the development team were finishing breakfast when a marketing person asked her what one additional feature they could incorporate to make her life easier. When she gave an "incremental" answer—make settlement a little cheaper—a programmer on the team asked if the team could return with her to her office and watch how she started her day. It turned out that Alice spent a full half of her day (1) printing out settlement statements from her vendors; (2) entering the printed data into three different in-house programs for accounting, settlement, and risk analysis; and (3) error checking her reports for any input problems. With less than one day's effort the programmer was able to implement straight-through processing, so that the data from the new service were automatically entered into the firm's three programs before Alice even came to work in the morning—reducing errors and eliminating nearly four hours of boring repetitive work each day!

Why had Alice not suggested help with the input procedure? Remember that she was extremely open and supportive of the new service. She was *unable* to suggest automatic straight-through processing because she did not know it was possible. Without the office visit the development team would not have included a feature in the first version of the service that made it very competitive with the market leaders.

Henry Ford understood the issue of customers not understanding the possibilities: "If I had asked people what they wanted, they would have said faster horses." Ford did not listen to the customers, which allowed his company to take the market leading spot in the United States. However, GM later overtook Ford using a customer-oriented strategy with the motto "a car for every purse and purpose,"[6] developing products for each distinct market segment. This illustrates a distinction between radical and incremental innovations. Ford was alone in the beginning and created something new. Asking customers would not have led to an expressed need

---

[6] Fullerton, R.A. 1988. "How Modern is Modern Marketing? Marketing's Evolution and the Myth of the "Production Era"." *The Journal of Marketing* pp. 108–125.

for a car; thus, they had to work in a more proactive manner. Henry Ford most likely realized the importance of personal transport by observing and understanding his contemporary environment. GM could later take advantage when the car had become an established product in society, and enabled further development, albeit via incremental methods.

The last category of methods in Table 3.1 is what we may call proactive methods—methods involving understanding the customers' actions carried out in their own context. These methods are more forward thinking and better served for more innovative or radical service innovations based on ideas submitted by customers. The lead user method attempts to find solutions that may have already been developed by customers. The previously mentioned examples—coffee filter, chocolate chip cookies, Frisbees, and so on—are all solutions developed by customers. One closely related method is enhanced customer involvement by giving users access to tools to modify the companies' services or products during their use. This effectively provides customers a platform on which they can test ideas with the purpose of encouraging the development of solutions they may find useful.

In-depth interviews and observation conducted at a user site advocated as "Voice of the Customer" research are an improvement on surveys or group methods for user insights and innovation ideas.[7] Ethnographic studies go further in pursuing a deep understanding of needs and uses. An ethnographic study will systematically map user behavior and identify routine behaviors users and customers employ in different situations. New concepts are then developed from these studies to support the customers' regular behavior and to enforce whatever the companies want to achieve in specific situations. Ethnographic studies have been used to design airplane gates to create more orderly aircraft boarding and the counters at McDonald's have been studied to provide a better customer experience. (The lead user method, customer involvement, and ethnographical studies are further described in Chapter 5.) Let us exemplify the overall complexity of the aforementioned by quoting Toyota's chief designer Kevin Hunter:

---

[7] Griffin, A., and J.R. Hauser. 1993. "The Voice of the Customer." *Marketing Science* 12, no. 1, pp. 1–27.

People can't tell you what they want in the future, but they know what they want now. You have to balance creativity with market acceptability. You have to push the envelope and be progressive, but you can't get too far out there, because customers won't understand. Your design has to evoke something familiar or emotional while at the same time offering something new and unfamiliar. You have to avoid a strict design bias and remember who you're designing for. You can't be selfish, you must focus outward, and on the problem you're trying to solve for customers.[8]

Multiple case studies have shown a positive impact from proactive user research tools on product innovation. A 2007 study of innovation in financial services at 211 banks examined proactive and traditional market research tools as constructs that defined the type of user knowledge driving service innovation. Each construct had six items. "Proactive Methods" comprised ethnography, user testing, site visits, lead user methods, in-depth onsite interviews, and voice of the customer (interviews and observation stressing context). "Tradition methods" comprised focus groups, group brainstorming, trade-off analysis, web surveys, test marketing, and concept testing. The study found that both the proactive and traditional user research constructs were antecedents of service innovation success, but *the use of proactive methods had more effect on the success of more innovative and radical service innovation.*

Building Your Own Market Competence!

We started this chapter asking who in *your* organization collects customer knowledge and what your organization does with the knowledge. When we ask these questions the answers are often vague; it seems that companies often rely either on intuition or market research from consultants who interpret the customers' needs and the information for them. We believe that it is important for organizations to develop competency and be

---

[8] May, M.E. November 16, 2013. "When It Pays to Listen to Users ... and When It Doesn't." *Innovation Excellence* (blog). www.innovationexcellence.com/blog/2013/11/16/when-it-pays-to-listen-to-users-and-when-it-doesnt

involved in user research. Is customer information not the most important data for a company?

Why is in-house customer knowledge so important? Hiring market survey consultants will convey *their* interpretation of the customers' views and needs. Customer information is often extensive; so consultants filter and edit information to be manageable, without having full knowledge of the company's industry segment. The company never has full knowledge of the customer.

In theoretical terms, the development of a service can be viewed as a matching process: The company should be able to develop a solution that corresponds to deep customer needs. The matching is carried out in a constantly evolving environment because of the constantly evolving customer needs, market activity, and technology. How well companies handle this matching depends on how well they can interpret explicit, tactic, and contextual user needs and deliver value to the customer.

Successfully managing this process requires relevant information and knowledge. We encourage questioning the role of external parties during this matching; it is important that the evaluators of customer information themselves have deep knowledge of the organization and its customers. Without a deep understanding, the distortion of information in this multistage process can be similar to outcomes in the familiar children's game "Chinese whispers" or "Telephone." Lack of insight into how the results have been acquired or how they should be interpreted causes problems, even in the early stages of collecting and sorting information. Don't outsource customer awareness.

Having company employees gather customer information themselves will automatically give the data collected a higher priority than if it has been purchased from an external source. Even the article cited earlier about the ineffectiveness of group research does note that one advantage of the group processes is that all the participants *believe* in the results. Spreading information and ensuring other employees are aware of it become a part of daily operations if employees are involved in conducting the research. The most common obstacle for companies aiming to become more customer oriented is not difficulties in acquiring information and understanding what customers want, but, rather, using it during the development process. Thus, implementing customer information is more difficult than acquiring; so third-party research can be wasteful in many ways.

One additional warning: Some market survey consultants apply existing solutions to corporate problems by developing one type of research method and a relatively standardized process or survey to apply to everyone. Some agencies specialize in customer surveys; others in so-called mystery shopping; and others in focus groups. Agencies improve their business efficiency by scaling up their solutions. This endangers the whole idea of service innovation, namely to cultivate knowledge about customers' value-creating processes. As a company, being aware of these phenomena and outlining the right requirements entails cultivating in-house competence at least sufficiently to manage agencies and consultants effectively. Having companies establish adequate levels of user research skills forces consultants to improve what they offer. This should actually be a mutually beneficial development. In studies of innovation success, knowledge of customer needs often appears as the single most critical component when launching new services.

We wish to point out that we have met many extremely driven and talented consultants in user research (and have done some consulting ourselves!) and we are not questioning the competence of all consultants— we simply feel that customer knowledge has to be regarded as a key competence for all companies. If a company does not know what its customers want, how is it going to deliver it to them?

Customer Orientation

Customer orientation can be described as a recurring process in which an organization (1) gathers customer information, (2) distributes the information, and (3) implements changes in existing products and services.[9] It is crucial to prepare the organization for responding to customer information and for translating customer needs into business activities. This consists of ensuring that work procedures and methods capable of handling the customers' needs are in place. Some kind of infrastructure is also needed in order for customer orientation to have an impact on daily operations, in the form of forums where the customers' needs and

[9] Jaworski, B.J., and A.K. Kohli. 1993. "Market Orientation: Antecedents and Consequences." *The Journal of Marketing* 57, pp. 53–70.

experiences may be discussed; resources required to implement changes; or improvement groups.

A company's customer-oriented service activities are characterized by the behavior of its coworkers. A company may have a customer-oriented strategy, but failing to support with the proper analytical work procedures, decision making, and implementation based on customer information will prevent the strategy from being more than well-written documents. Companies often understand the importance of working toward customer satisfaction, yet lack the requisite work procedures for carrying out the said work practically. An organization that fails to distribute and implement this increased knowledge of the customers' needs and expectations will forfeit the impact it would otherwise have on daily operations, resulting in a customer-oriented organization only by name and not by action.

One of the primary goals of genuinely customer-oriented companies is good customer experiences and refined methods for gathering and analyzing customer information used in daily operations. One important question for companies to ask is to what extent such user research and action actually occurs and, consequently, to what extent they operate as genuinely customer-oriented companies.

Breaking Habitual Patterns

It is difficult for a company to become more customer orientated; old habits are hard to break. Carrying out tasks in a new way consumes more time and there is no guarantee that the results will be satisfactory on the initial try.

A research study performed by John Ettlie and Michael Johnson showed that when a new customer-orientation method was introduced, the organization actually became less customer oriented the first time the method was used. This phenomenon was explained by the organization focusing on the method itself and not on its purpose, which is to understand the customers' needs.[10] It should also be mentioned that there is no guarantee that an organization will be able to correctly identify

---

[10] Ettlie, J.E., and M.D. Johnson. 1994. "Product Development Benchmarking Versus Customer Focus in Applications of Quality Function Deployment." *Marketing Letters* 5, no. 2, pp. 107–16.

existing work procedures and routines. External competencies, such as consultants assisting in customer-orientation assessments, could be useful in that case. (See we have nothing against consultants!)

An example can be found in a difficult period for Volvo Cars. In the beginning of the 90s, Volvo was in dire straits. Despite continuously improving cars, it fell further down the rankings in JD Power's surveys on customer opinions of car makes. JD Power carries out one of the car industry's most important global surveys and measures customer opinions of all makes available on the American market. The reason for Volvo's drop in the rankings was its excessive focus on internal processes—improving productivity—which failed to include customers and competitors in the product and process improvements. Quality-improvement procedures were purely internally focused.

Volvo adopted externally focused quality-improvement procedures to restore balance in the company. A new strategy with increased customer satisfaction as the primary goal was deployed, leading to a change in work procedures. Volvo started carrying out more customer research, made customer information available to everyone in the organization, and began communicating customer needs internally, even including dealerships in the process. Within a few years, Volvo reaped the benefits in the form of higher customer satisfaction and increased revenue. In conclusion, Volvo managed to change its behavior, but a crisis was needed to break a habitual pattern.

The difficulty in breaking habitual patterns also appears in research studies. One oft-referenced study showed significantly improved products and financial results of an IT company that implemented work procedures to promote increased use of customer opinions. However, despite this evidence, that company chose to return to the old and familiar work procedures because the new methods required too great an effort to achieve a permanent change! The staff did not feel confident in working with the new procedures and simply preferred the old ones.

In our work with companies, we have often encountered people claiming "that's how we've always done it," "we've never done that," or "that probably works there, but not here—we really are unique." The pejorative term Not Invented Here ("NIH"), a suspicion of external ideas, is another force reinforcing inertia in an organization. It is simply not as stimulating to work with an idea that has been conceived by someone else, which is why external ideas and information are often rejected. Research shows that the NIH syndrome may potentially lead to innovations with low customer value and a tendency to reinvent the wheel. The expression "proudly found elsewhere" has been created as a counter movement to the NIH syndrome.

Customer-Oriented Companies of the Future

A true customer orientation is a competitive advantage for a firm. But are most organizations ready for customer orientation? Different types of specializations in organization operations in terms of their stance on customer information are available in Figure 3.2.

Companies used to do well by offering only one good product as long as there was a market for it. Companies have basically relied on finding market channels and marketing the product at the right price. The so-called market mix in accordance with the 4P model has, as such, helped companies to offer their product on the right market at the right price, represented by the top row in Figure 3.2.

Global competition has changed the situation however—one good product is not sufficient to survive, forcing organizations to become more market oriented. Market orientation requires companies to learn more about markets and customers in order to adapt their actions accordingly. This creates markets where companies largely follow each other and segment customers in similar manners. This is represented by the middle row in Figure 3.2.

True competitiveness requires customer orientation. Even though customer orientation is viewed as a component of market orientation, there are some important distinctions between market-oriented and customer-oriented organizations. Market orientation also focuses more on internal and competitor activities and is consequently based on the activities of a range of actors on the market. Customer orientation focuses on in-depth knowledge of the customers and their problems as well as how the company builds relations with its customers. Customer orientation involves tailoring actions according to customers' market activities and thought processes.

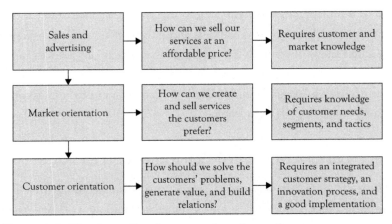

Figure 3.2 The interrelated nature of market and customer orientation

Offering a good product or service may have been sufficient at one time, but due to heightened competitions this is not the case anymore. The primary task of a company and its employees should be to help solve the customers' problems, which requires close customer proximity and an understanding of their actions carried out in their own context. This development is described in the following way by William Clay Ford Jr., great grandson of Henry Ford:

> If you go back to even a very short while ago, our whole idea of a customer was that we would wholesale a car to a dealer, the dealer would then sell the car to the customer, and we hoped we never heard from the customer—because if we did, it meant something was wrong.

> Today we want to establish a dialogue with the customer throughout the entire ownership experience. We want to talk to and touch our customers at every step of the way. We want to be a consumer products and services company that just happens to be in the automotive business.[11]

---

[11] Garten, J.E. 2008. *The Mind of the CEO*, 139. New York: Basic Books.

Even though the quote is in reference to Ford, it applies to other companies as well. The Swedish company SKF, for instance, specializes in ball bearings, but so do other companies as well. What SKF truly excels in is—in somewhat simplified terms—how ball bearings should be mounted and their operational conditions. The first-mentioned example is an expression of market orientation, while the last-mentioned one represents customer orientation. Claiming that customers are important and placing them at the center of corporate strategies is a taken for granted in many companies, but the important question to ask is how these words can be turned into actions.

The two most recent meta-analyses of antecedents of new product success have shown customer orientation to be a consistent primary success predictor. Using a standard construct to define customer orientation, a study of service innovation in banks unsurprisingly found that customer orientation was a significant antecedent of service innovation success for the banks. The *effect size*, 0.22, was large. This effect size roughly indicates that nearly a quarter of the variation in the success of the service innovation could be explained by the degree of customer orientation within a bank.[12]

Summary

Organizations that want to be successful in service innovation should (1) develop proficiency in user research, and (2) strive to develop a true customer orientation. Organizations should particularly focus on using proactive user research tools.

Focusing on value-creating processes, that is, understanding the customers' wishes and facilitating their everyday activities, requires a deep understanding of their daily life and behavioral patterns. This information is not easily acquired, due to the difficulty in understanding the value of "sticky," "contextual," and latent knowledge and information, which, in turn, makes it difficult to transfer. Conquering this challenge requires putting the customers in the driver's seat and letting them lead part of the

---

[12] Schirr, G.R., and A.L. Page. 2009. "Antecedents of Service Development Success: A Culture-Tools-Process Model." *American Marketing Association Winter Conference 2009*, p. 27, eds. F.L. Tampa, K. Reynolds, and J. Chris White.

development. Entire organizations might also have to be rewired to enable new ways of absorbing and distributing customer information, which, in particular, highlights how important customer information is in an organization—the absence of customer information will make it difficult to understand how a company can support its customers' processes.

Action questions for the service innovator:

- What is your assessment of *your* employees' level of knowledge of customers and users?
- Who in your organization observes users creating value with your services?
- How is the knowledge gained (1) saved and (2) put to work?
- If someone contacts your organization to tell you how to improve your services, how will your organization respond?
- What is the ratio between the amount of time spent on internal organization processes and the time spent on understanding the customers' value-generating processes?
- Is your organization truly "customer oriented" (or user oriented)?

The main sources of inspiration for this chapter are:

The following articles respectively capture service innovation together with the customer, the ability of organizations to capture external information, different methods for customer interaction in development processes, communication in innovation processes, the importance of "sticky" information, and, finally, the importance of employees.

Alam, I. 2002. "An Exploratory Investigation of User Involvement in New Service Development." *Journal of the Academy of Marketing Science* 30, no. 3, pp. 250–61.

Cadwallader, S., C. Jarvis, M. Bitner, and A. Ostrom. 2010. "Frontline Employee Motivation to Participate in Service Innovation Implementation." *Journal of the Academy of Marketing Science* 38, no. 2, pp. 219–39.

Cohen, W.M., and D.A. Levinthal. 1990. "Absorptive Capacity: A New Perspective on Learning and Innovation." *Administrative Science Quarterly* 35, no. 1, pp. 128–52.

Edvardsson, B., P. Kristensson, P. Magnusson, and E. Sundström. 2012. "Customer Integration Within Service Development: A Review of Methods and an Analysis of In Situ and Ex Situ Contributions." *Technovation* 32, no. 7, pp. 419–29.

Engen, M., and P.R. Magnusson. 2015. "Exploring the Role of Frontline Employees as Innovators." *The Service Industries Journal* 35, no. 6, pp. 303–24.

Ettlie, J.E., and M.D. Johnson. 1994. "Product Development Benchmarking Versus Customer Focus in Applications of Quality Function Deployment." *Marketing Letters* 5, no. 2, pp. 107–16.

Gustafsson, A., P. Kristensson, and L. Witell. 2012. "Customer Co-Creation in Service Innovation: A Matter of Communication?" *Journal of Service Management* 23, no. 3, pp. 311–27.

Schirr, G.R. 2012. "Flawed Tools: The Efficacy of Group Research Methods to Generate Customer Ideas." *Journal of Product Innovation Management* 29, no. 3, pp. 473–88.

Skålén, P. 2010. "Service Marketing and Subjectivity: The Shaping of Customer-Oriented Employees." *Journal of Marketing Management* 25, no. 7–8, pp. 795–809.

von Hippel, E. 1994. "'Sticky Information' and the Locus of Problem Solving: Implications for Innovation." *Management Science* 40, no. 4, pp. 429–39.

We also refer to closely related areas such as market orientation, which, in actual fact, constitutes an entirely separate theory. More information on market orientation is available in:

Narver, J.C., and S.F. Slater. 1990. "The Effect of a Market Orientation on Business Profitability." *Journal of Marketing* 54, no. 4, pp. 20–35.

We have also referenced some case descriptions:

Flodin, S., T. Nelson, and A. Gustafsson. 1997. "Improved Customer Satisfaction Is a Volvo Priority." In *Customer Retention in the Automotive Industry,* eds. I.M. Johnson, A. Herrmann, F. Huber, and A. Gustafsson. Wiesbaden: Gabler.

Olson, E.L., and G. Bakke. 2001. "Implementing the Lead User Method in a High Technology Firm: A Longitudinal Study of Intentions Versus Actions." *Journal of Product Innovation Management* 18, no. 6, pp. 388–95.

CHAPTER 4

Developing Service Innovations

The process of new service development is not well defined, and does not adhere to conventional empirical mechanisms. Yet, new services come onto the market every day. "How?" remains the critical question.
— Martin and Horne (1993, 62)[1]

This chapter covers the service innovation process and the steps that we feel an organization must successfully carry out in order to create a complete offering. Service innovation is more iterative and less structured than product-development processes for goods. Our suggestion will be that a service innovation process in essence is divided into three steps: focus (on the development project), understand (the customer), and build (a structure that facilitates delivery of customer value). However, we do expand on likely content in each step. One oft-voiced concern about service innovation is that services are easier and quicker to copy than physical products. Therefore, the chapter concludes with a discussion of the ways in which a company can create unique offerings.

Preview of Action Questions

- How and when does your organization involve customers or users in your service innovation process?
- Is your firm able to test and experiment with new services in real environments?

---

[1] Martin, C.R., and D.A. Horne. 1993. "Services Innovation: Successful Versus Unsuccessful Firms." *International Journal of Service Industry Management* 4, no. 1, pp. 49–64.

Service Innovation as a Process

Comparing service innovation processes with new product-development processes for goods reveals that the former are often less structured and not as well documented. Data we have collected reveal that structured development processes can be found in only about half of all service companies.

Even this 50 percent assumption may be overstated: One of the authors asked a group of service innovators if they had a formal service innovation process in place. He followed up with individual interviews of the ones who said that they did have a formal process in place and had them describe their most recent innovation in detail. It turned out that the majority of the service innovators, in this small sample, who said that they had a formal process in place had not actually followed the described formal structure in their most recent new service development! It seemed that some of the service innovators *wanted* to have a structured process but were unable to apply a process originally developed for new product development of goods to more iterative service innovation.

In our encounters with companies, we are often told of how services have been developed around the coffee table or, as was the case with text messaging—short messaging service (SMS; described in the previous chapter), over a pint of beer and a pizza, that is, basically anywhere but the company's conference rooms. Research also shows that companies that invest in development and employ structured processes enjoy a greater hit rate, more satisfied customers, and higher profitability. This suggests that we should consider the components required to develop successful service innovations.

Innovations have different degrees of novelty as defined, for example, by the incremental, more innovative, radical classification scheme described in Chapter 2. As in goods innovation, the majority of service innovations are incremental, modifying existing offerings with the purpose of increasing company competitiveness. Incremental development work should be an optimization effort—how a company can increase its competitiveness by creating a better offering, and thereby enjoy more loyal customers. Incremental efforts must be focused on areas with the greatest potential for impact as resources are limited. Research shows that efficient incremental innovation involves communicating with customers, involving them in the entire development process. An incremental innovation represents current customer needs and changes that a customer can easily understand.

As noted in Chapter 3, communication is a complex and multifaceted phenomenon. We define customer communication in terms of: (1) *frequency*, which denotes how often a company meets its customers in different forums; (2) *direction*, which indicates whether or not customer and company meet on equal terms or if there is any kind of balance of power at play; (3) *medium*, the way communication is carried out; and, finally, (4) the *content* of the discussion, which includes the level of detail in the solutions that the customer may provide.[2]

A successful incremental service innovation depends on the communication with customers during the development work. The most successful companies carry out frequent meetings with their customers. Research also indicates that it is important that the company and customer meet on equal terms. Content of the meetings is important: Firms should encourage customers to provide concrete proposals and solutions, as well as problems and perceived needs. Our research finds, however, that one of the facets of communication, the choice of medium, does not have any direct impact on the service innovation outcome.

In summary, a company should spend a great deal of time with its customers in their own context in order to succeed in service innovation. What applies to people also applies to people in companies: The more you interact, the better you will know each other. Encourage the customers to talk about solutions and new services. Experiment with a variety of different media to communicate: *Our research indicates that interacting via social media, forums, or blogs may work as well in some cases as interacting face to face.*

The biggest innovation challenge is the third category, radical innovation, which requires substantial customer interaction and familiarity with customer context in order to acquire tacit, latent, context-specific

[2] Gustafsson, A., P. Kristensson, and L. Witell. 2012. "Customer Co-Creation in Service Innovation: A Matter of Communication?" *Journal of Service Management* 23, no. 3, pp. 311–27.

information. Context is key to revealing customers' latent needs. Two approaches to uncover this difficult-to-gather information are (1) proactive user research, which was discussed in Chapter 3, and (2) active customer involvement in innovation, which is discussed in Chapter 5.

For many companies there seems to be no shortage of customer information. CRM systems record all the contacts or "touches" between the customer and customer service, sales, and researchers. In addition, smart companies conduct ongoing customer and user research, incorporating the proactive tools and the customer involvement techniques of Chapters 3 and 5. The problem faced by many companies is finding a way to prioritize customer information and decide what is important and how to use it, or deciding what problems or needs to focus on and how to use whatever limited resources are at hand.

Our prescription is focus: understand the customer and establish a structure for service innovation. One suggestion of a service innovation process can be found in Figure 4.1. The process described in the figure is not meant to be a strict linear progression nor should you think that you need to follow each and every step. An organization using a structured linear process, such as a Stage-Gate® approach to new product development, will likely need to modify the process for service innovation.

Our research shows that the development process structure in successful service companies is lenient and iterative. Service innovation projects alternate between phases to a higher degree than in new product development for goods. However, it is useful to highlight the important components of successful service innovation processes from our studies.

Figure 4.1 has been divided into three major phases: focus (focus) during the development project, understanding (understand) the customer, and establishing (establish) a structure that facilitates the delivery of customer value. Interestingly "design thinking," which focuses on deep knowledge of customers and iteration, also breaks the innovation into three processes—inspiration, ideation, and implementation.[3] The service innovation model we have observed and advocate shares features with the design thinking approach.

---

[3] Brown, T. 2009. *Change by Design*, ed. B. Katz, 16. New York: Harper Business.

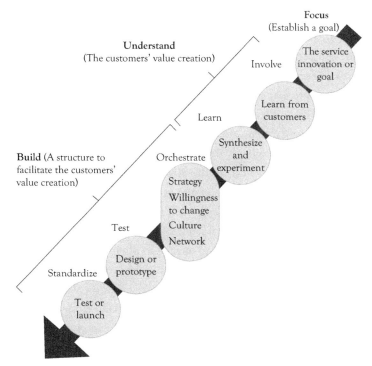

Figure 4.1 The service innovation development process

In the focus–understand–build model, the two latter phases are segmented into additional activities to better understand the activities required for service innovation success, resulting in six steps in total. The full process is illustrated in Figure 4.1, which was drawn to go downward from right to left, reflecting the outward to inward flow of the process: the original focus is outside the organization or from the customer perspective.

Phase I: Focus

The first step of the service innovation process is to establish a goal of what kind of value-creation process to develop. Which of the main value-creation process types described in Chapter 2 shall be improved: stream-line, differentiate, helping, or experience? Companies and organizations should not use an excessively broad scope during their development process; they should focus on the customers' "jobs." A specific goal makes it easier to understand what resources should be integrated in order to provide the best possible solutions for the customers. Focus also makes it easier to understand what needs to be studied.

It is possible that a company, after identifying its area of focus, could find an already implemented solution, perhaps in a different industry or another country. One such example is the prepaid card for mobile phones, which was originally developed by the Irish operator Eircell (now known as Vodafone Ireland) in the 90s to allow new customer groups to make phone calls. The card was aimed at individuals who, for various reasons, were not eligible for permanent mobile phone subscriptions, perhaps due to a lack of a regular income, being underage, missing identity documents, or needing privacy to engage in illicit activities. The concept became an immediate success despite the higher cost.

Another way of finding the goals an organization should outline is to study the areas from which innovations normally emerge in a particular industry. Have the innovations consisted of experiences, processes, or financing? If so, it could indicate what customers generally perceive as important. Is it possible to find a completely new niche? This could involve areas where no previous innovation activities have taken place. A company that has always focused on hardware or is operating in an industry that focuses on goods may want to consider service innovations.

Another method to identify goals is to make long-term trend analyses where companies try to predict the direction their industry is heading. For instance, Posten (the Swedish postal service) has for a long time predicted that its customers will prefer electronic correspondence to traditional letters. Consequently, Posten has developed solutions that combine web-based services with regular postcards. Posten is seeking business solutions in a market facing a steady decline in letters and postcards sent each year.

Phase II: Understand

The phase following focus is understand. Achieving understanding of the customers' value-creation process can be thought of as two steps: involving customers in innovation and learning from them.

Involve

Involving customers facilitates learning both from and with the customers. As previously pointed out, this learning process ideally takes place in the customer's own context and does not rely solely on memory-based research methods such as focus groups or surveys.

Ethnographical studies or methods based on active customer involvement have proven to work best. One example of customer involvement was the development of Volvo XC90. Rich married women in California, also known as "Hollywood wives," were regarded as the main customer group and Volvo focused on involving them in the development process. From detailed knowledge of how the car was to be used by these potential customer, Volvo was able to discover solutions that would not have been possible if development had been carried out internally without customer involvement.[4]

Service innovation consists of "discovering" customer experiences, which are improved to create satisfied customers. However, the journey of discovery has a far less certain outcome than it would appear to have when completed. The task of the developing party is to help the customers communicate information on what creates actual value and to solve the problems at hand. A company can more easily understand how to negotiate this challenge by involving customers or studying them in their natural environment.

Learn

It is not always easy for companies to translate customer needs into a saleable product. Good innovations not only create opportunities for new values for the customer but also contribute to long-term corporate profitability. In the learning phase, the company must learn as much as possible about the customers and their contexts. A key issue for the company is how to transform this customer information into a solution capable of

---

[4] Dahlsten, F. 2004. "Hollywood Wives Revisited: A Study of Customer Involvement in the XC90 Project at Volvo Cars." *European Journal of Innovation Management* 44, no. 2, pp. 141–49.

being internalized and realized in a reasonable manner despite imperfect knowledge of what customers want and how willing they are to pay for a solution. One high-level manager at an innovative company described this issue in the following way:

> Customers always have lots of requests and when we ask them if they want us to come up with a solution to a problem the answer generally is yes—however, when the solution is ready, it turns out very few customers are willing to adopt it or pay for it.

The manager's interpretation of the situation is that the customers are not telling the truth, which is probably not the case. Customers may give their best prediction, but predicting needs for new solutions is very difficult. Customers might believe that a particular solution has some kind of practical value in its unrealized state, only to discover that it is not as useful the case when given the opportunity to try it. Therefore, it is wise to test a potential solution as soon as possible.

The company may start by outlining simple solutions that can be tested on employees or users in order to be as realistic as possible. The work group can enact scenarios to get indications of whether or not they are on the right track. Some companies use customer panels to discuss various solutions while some use a particular market as a "test market" to implement pilot projects and relevant solutions. Rapid prototyping can push this process along.

A major fear in this situation is that a company's competitors will find out the direction it is heading. These concerns are well founded in service innovation; services are easily copied. However, it is difficult for a competitor to identify and understand the plethora of services offered by a competing. Confidentiality is not an insurmountable problem if a company has found a market-relevant solution capable of being implemented in the organization with reasonable resource use. The company should always be one step ahead of its competitors in innovation, which will allow them to more quickly introduce further new services. If they stay on top of customer information, the company that launched a new service should be first to market with versions 2.0 and 3.0!

A high-level manager at Volvo Cars said that Volvo has traditionally been good at maintaining confidentiality and curtailing the dissemination of internal information. However, the restrictions on dissemination of information were so severe that it did not even reach key company employees. He went on to state that if the need exists, competitors will be able to obtain any kind of internal information regardless of what security measures are in place. He concluded that the benefits of spreading customer information internally outweighed the competitive drawbacks. In reply to the information problem, Volvo created a database—the Volvo Index of Car Experience (VOICE)—and made it available internally to everyone at the company, which was one of the factors for the company's success at the end of the 90s.

Phase III: Build

After the understand phase we move into an build phase that includes the steps—orchestrate, test, and standardize. The build phase needs to be convergent and move toward a solution to the identified problem.

Orchestrate

In the orchestrate phase, the company faces crossroads in implementing the new solution. It is crucial to stop and reflect on how realistic the solution is and how difficult or easy it will be to implement. The company must take several factors into account: How aligned is the solution with the company's strategy? Will the organization be able to carry out necessary changes? Will the organization be able to sustain the new service? And finally, will the company's business relationship network be able to support the new innovation?

Few organizations sell one single service—rather, they sell "bundles" of services that are aimed at facilitating customers' everyday activities and solving their problems. In goods it is not uncommon to have one stand-alone product; this is rare for services. A company may regard its range of services as a system of integrated components whose purpose is to deliver value to the customer. This can be exemplified by observing telecommunications companies that deliver offers such as fixed telephony, broadband, mobile phone, and IP TV services to its customers. In some cases, these types of enterprises are composed of different organizational units for each individual service as well as different customer service departments with individual opening hours. If the same company delivers all these services, customers will not regard them as separate entities—they contact the company to get help and do not care if the problem with their TV is caused by the broadband connection or the IP TV itself. The different segments must not cancel each other out however, as the company strategy has to encompass the offer in its entirety. One possible solution is to implement IP telephony despite its effect on the other segments (fixed and mobile telephony usage may decrease, while broadband usage may increase). Sometimes we speak in terms of channels that companies use to reach a certain market. The customers, however, do not distinguish between channels—as far as they are concerned they are dealing with a single company. Customer service in a company using different channels must be able to cover the gaps between channels in order to appear seamless; the customer must not be able to detect any channel switching at all if the experience is to be successful. All contact with a company must be convenient and coordinated.

Corporate culture is incredibly complex; not all cultures are capable of delivering certain types of service successfully. An organization is often focused on delivering a service as efficiently as possible. A focus on efficiency and a development phase that has most likely taken a long time can create norms and values in terms of how organizational members should act. People find it difficult to break habits: Norms and values can be regarded as aggregated habits and their advantage is their ability to enable efficiency improvement—a task that has been carried out before does not require much effort to be carried out again.

Look back at how it felt when learning to drive a car compared to how it feels now—a process that we have mastered becomes second nature. Given new services, companies must ask themselves if the organization will be able to break existing norms or if it would be better to simply avoid implementing the new service altogether. In fact, a better option might be to start a new organization in parallel with the old one in order to deliver a new offering.

A famous example of the need for a new organization was the IBM PC. After being late to market with midrange computers, IBM decided that it had to be a leader in the new personal computer market. However, IBM executives knew that their engineering department's emphasis on performance and their marketing department's fear of cannibalization of profitable products would hinder—or more likely, kill—any PC project. So IBM created a new entity located in Boca Raton, Florida, far away from its New York headquarters, that successfully launched the PC in 1981.

Many goods-based organizations today stand at a crossroads in terms of whether to deliver more services. Research shows that offering service presents an inherent problem caused by company cultures not ready for change. Company staffs may be comfortable accepting orders from customers via item numbers, receiving the order, and dispatching goods from a central warehouse. When delivering services, the staff may need to travel to the customers in order to find out what problem needs to be solved, design a specific solution to the problem, and subsequently coordinate with a number of suppliers to make the customer satisfied. This constitutes an entirely new way of working, which becomes a difficult challenge. Researchers sometimes recommend not making this change to existing organizations but rather to create a specific department in parallel with the existing organization. When the new department's revenue reaches a benchmark such as 10 or 20 percent of the total revenue, it is deemed sufficiently large to handle the internal competition and may subsequently be merged with the rest of the organization.

Some organizations may find it difficult to implement solutions that involve solving individual customer problems since they lack the requisite level of customer orientation. Other organizations that are by tradition built on customer interaction have exceptionally skilled employees who are able to attend to the customers in an exemplary manner. It might be difficult for such organizations to implement new technical solutions both from the customers' and the employees' perspectives.

The Swedish Social Insurance Agency is an example of an organization that has suffered from such problems. Their strategy has long been based on letting the insured parties solve the more trivial problems themselves via technical solutions so that employees may focus on more complex problems. The challenge for the social insurance agency has been its relatively low level of technological maturity that has made it difficult to fully implement various information technology (IT) solutions designed to support customers.

Since services are coproduced with customers, distributing them can be a challenge. If a company operates on a global market, it is wise to establish a relationship or network with other companies that assist in delivering services directly to the customer. Not even a company the size of IBM or Ericsson is able to use in-house staff in every location where their product is offered. If one of their customers requests service of a product, the company must have someone ready on site who can quickly help the customer, which may require sending another company to represent it.

Test

The next step is to extract feasible concepts in the customers' contexts. This must be carried out in close collaboration with selected customers in order to allow the company to tailor solutions to specific customers and customer groups. For industrial companies, this involves working symbiotically with customers with whom they have a good relationship and for whom they are developing a concept that meets specific needs. For companies in the consumer market industry, this process relies on a testing market or office where the new concept can be launched initially. The concept of first implementing a service or product in a limited market is based on being able to test a solution on a small scale before making a more extensive and costly change.

Standardize

The last phase in the model consists of launching a new service on an open market. A number of service modifications probably have taken place during the test phase, which means that the company might not be able to offer the service to all customers. In order to launch the service on a larger scale, some segments have to be standardized to allow delivery to a greater number of customers as uniformly as possible. It is simply too expensive to offer custom-made solutions to every single customer.

Volvo Trucks have found a creative solution to the problem of standardization. They bundle their solutions by packaging services and giving them an item number as if they were regular products. In the consumer market, Geek Squad sells standardized service "packages" for protection of computers or related technical goods.

Several companies in the more traditional service sector also employ this "package" strategy. The financial services industry has long attempted to standardize financial and nonfinancial services. Components of service "productification" include employee outfits, the store environment, service brochures, and the company's logo.

Service Innovation Implementation

Identifying all the important phases of service innovation implementation would likely fill another book. We argue that the greatest service implementation challenge lies in rolling out the new innovation to customers via company staff. Company staff must embrace the service and promote it in such a way that customers will purchase it, and then deliver the service in such a way that customers are delighted.

The new service innovation will ideally be intuitive and easy to understand for both customers and company staff. Moreover, services are seldom offered individually, but are usually incorporated into what we previously referred to as a bundle and must therefore be compatible with other products and services. It might take some time before the services can be merged into a single entity. The corollary to this strong reliance on staff and the single web of services is that the implementation time of service innovation may be greater than that of product innovation.

The development time for a service innovation can in fact appear relatively short in relation to implementation time. The reader might recall how long it took from the time when online banking was first introduced until a majority of customers chose to adopt this service innovation. The development time in this case was significantly shorter than the adoption time.

We would also like to emphasize a few aspects that companies may need to focus on in order to succeed during implementation:

1. Share information that is important to you. How should the company express values addressed by the new service innovation that are important to the company and its customers?
2. Enable customers to adapt the service to their own needs. There are numerous advantages involved when customers are able to adapt solutions to their own needs. This, in particular, solves more of the customers' latent needs; however, it also makes it difficult for them to replace services. If possible, the solution should be a platform for value-creation that can be adapted to the customers' needs.
3. Adapt according to context. How should the company address specific user segments more directly in order to customize the offer to the customer? The company needs to be able to address its customers more directly and the first step is to identify the customer group in question.
4. Differentiate. How can the company discover unique properties that bind the solution together? To facilitate implementation, it is necessary to point out the services' unique properties to the customer compared to that of existing ones on the market.

How Unique Is Your Service Innovation?

As noted, a big problem with service innovations is that they can easily be copied, which requires companies to consider how unique their service innovation really is.

In Chapter 2, we presented a model that divides service innovations into six different categories: process innovation, brand innovation, business model innovation, experience innovation, social innovation, and behavioral innovation. These types of innovations must be aligned with the company's competence and resources. Business models are by nature difficult to copy since they mainly involve emphasizing a company's strengths and new ways of charging the customer, which is why we have chosen not to bring them up. Business model innovation will instead be discussed in Chapter 6.

Process Innovation

In general, the most easily copied type of service innovation is what we refer to as process innovation or streamline. The purpose of process innovation is to improve efficiency and thereby save resources—either the company's or the customer's. We could regard the concept of lean as a type of process innovation in which flows are optimized with regard to resource efficiency both for customers and companies. One distinguishing characteristic of process innovation is that it can be transferred to other companies and even to other contexts—in other words, it is not tied to a specific company or its customer relations.

In order for the companies to succeed with this type of service innovation, they must either have a strong customer base that can quickly embrace the solution or possess a sufficient amount of resources in order to withstand other companies that copy their concept. For example, Amazon has become so large and efficient at online retailing that new entrants to online retailing often find it attractive to be hosted by Amazon. The key to stymieing competition lies in being the largest actor on the market or having the strongest brand in combination with continuous reinvention procedures. One of the reasons why the founders of Skype decided to sell their company was that they feared a company with greater resources, such as Microsoft or Google—which already have strong existing customer bases and relations—would copy their idea, which would make it very difficult for Skype to survive in a long-term perspective.

Brand Innovation

Studying strong brands that are referred to as service innovations, such as Google, Starbucks, or Ikea, reveals that each represents arrays of innovations that collectively represent the actual service innovation. Even though each of these innovations can easily be copied individually, it is incredibly difficult to copy the entire concept.

Ikea is a good example. Figure 4.2 attempts to illustrate its core activities, where the darker colored activities are most important as they represent Ikea's areas of focus. The company is driven by a pervasive eagerness to constantly lower internal costs, which obviously includes its manufacturing process as well. Focusing on cost reduction has also had an impact

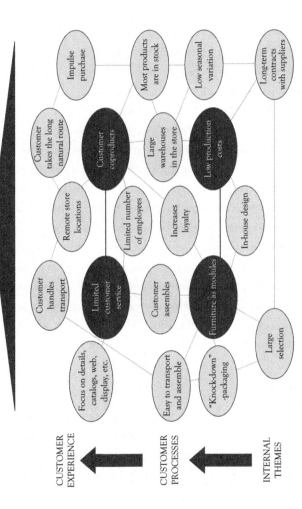

Figure 4.2 The core of Ikea's service[3]

[3] Gustafsson, A., and M.D. Johnson. 2003. *Competing in a Service Economy: How to Create a Competitive Advantage through Service Development and Innovation.* San Francisco, CA: Jossey-Bass.

on other areas that constitute key components in Ikea's innovation work. This has led to a module-based paradigm that allows identical components to be implemented in different applications. Ikea's customers are expected to contribute to the value-creating process to let it further circumscribe its costs. Ikea's coproduction and modularization of furniture allows it to limit its customer support, and its focus areas are surrounded by a number of service innovations that promote additional consolidation. The purpose of Figure 4.2 is to illustrate how Ikea's internal processes are used to support the customers' preferred actions in their interaction with it, which subsequently leads to customer experiences.

Another key principle illustrated in the figure is the interactivity linking aimed at achieving a "seamless" system. The innovations build on each other and make it easier for Ikea to deliver a complete solution to the customer.

Business Model Innovation

Replacing the business model of a particular service could either be a strategic decision that takes several years to complete or an everyday activity. The ease with which a business model can be created and introduced on a market depends on the level of cultural change required, both as far as the organization and the customers are concerned. A new business model that fits in well with the customers' value-creating processes has a greater chance for rapid deployment and market success.

The Internet has rendered previously chargeable services such as news subscriptions, matching services, and file storage nonchargeable since customers expect them to be offered for free. Today we visit sites like *The Wall Street Journal (WSJ)*, LinkedIn, and DropBox using services that are offered free of charge in a business model called "Freemium." A good basic service is available for free at these sites. But if you want something more—such as certain articles in the *WSJ*, better search or messaging on LinkedIn, or more storage on DropBox—you must pay for a subscription. When Chris Anderson wrote the book *Free—The Future of a Radical Price*, he posted an audiobook version on his blog, which was made available for free. However, the abridged version of the book containing only the most important sections was not available for free.

Companies like Google, Nintendo, and various social media platforms have all been able to reap great benefits from business model
innovations. For example, Google chose to give access to a great search
engine for free and earn money on advertising. Google applied the same
model when it entered the market for mobile phone operating systems,
with the result that Android has the dominant major share. The key for
successfully launching a new business model innovation is that both the
company and customer benefit from it.

Social Innovation

The purpose of social innovation is to be replicated by others since the
underlying ambition is based on social commitment and a belief in a
better society by providing help to those in need. We gave a few examples
of this type of innovation earlier in the book, such as "paused coffee,"
"layaway angels," and the concept of collecting equipment no longer used
by public actors and reselling it to other parties. One social innovation
currently enjoying significant growth is advanced education where new
and established actors alike (e.g., the edX collaboration led by Harvard
and MIT) are offering education for free.

Experience Innovation

In order to succeed in service innovation, the company has to be unique,
otherwise it will not be able to charge the price needed to cover costs
associated with niched services. One such example is that of Chuck E.
Cheese. Its concept is actually based on a regular pizzeria that has been
augmented to provide an exciting experience to small children where
they can interact with Chuck E. Cheese (a big mouse) and play lots of
different games on arcade machines. Coupons that can be used to claim
prizes are issued to customers who do well on these machines. Today's
market is saturated with experiences—who has not heard of bungee
jumping, zip lines, or indoor water parks? Unique customer experiences
is said to be one of the major remedies for brick and mortar stores against
Internet.

Behavioral Innovation

As previously mentioned, the purpose of behavioral innovation is to create a market and bring about a change in customer behavior. We have nevertheless chosen to view behavioral innovation as a special type of service innovation. The underlying objective is again to point out the importance of starting with the customers and their behavior as it constitutes the basis of service innovation. As pointed out in the introduction of this chapter, our view of innovation is based on starting at the market level and analyzing the customers' expectations of the value-creating processes. This is the diametrical opposite of an inward–outward paradigm, which starts with an innovation and then lets the customers contemplate what they are supposed to use it for. Iridium Satellite Phones, deliberately crashing a fleet of satellites, is a famous example of what happens to a great technical solution that does not have a market. Another extreme example of this phenomenon is the company Uddeholm, which developed a type of steel that was so hard that it was not possible to process with normal tools. Unfortunately, there was no real area of applicability either—Uddeholm did not know which customers would find any use for it or even if any areas of application existed. Eventually they did find use for the material in valves for extreme engins.

Behavioral innovation encompasses a process in which the customers must make radical changes to their way of acting in order to use the innovation. The company must consider how much it dares change the customers' behavior to, in effect, make the offer unique. One example of this phenomenon is Spotify. Its customers can basically ignore their collection of CDs as they have to adopt a completely new behavior in order to benefit from the company's services.

Considerable changes to customer behavior are very difficult to achieve, as the customers will demand significant benefits in return. One alternative to voluntary adoption is to force the customers to make the necessary changes. One example of the latter mentioned is the self-service concept found at airports where the airline does not accept customers unless they have already checked in themselves.

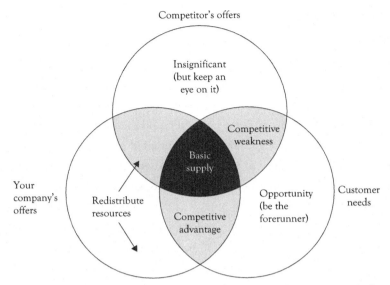

Figure 4.3 Which category best represents the service innovation?[5]

We would like to give the following advice to companies that want to evaluate how unique their service innovation really is: Consider which of the aforementioned categories of service innovation best represents the idea in question. Ideas that are not unique to the company's own customers, suppliers, and contexts are incidentally most easily copied by competitors, and experience shows that said services are most often based on process innovations that are aimed at improving efficiency.

Figure 4.3 illustrates another way of analyzing service innovation. The process begins by categorizing a company's current activities and competitors. Activities that are carried out in the same industry will most likely overlap while some aspects have to be unique in order to achieve a degree of differentiation. One question a company may ask itself is which category best represents the new innovation. Is it supposed to increase intercompany similarities or promote differentiation? The latter obviously

---

[5] Gustafsson, A., and M.D. Johnson. 2003. *Competing in a Service Economy: How to Create a Competitive Advantage through Service Development and Innovation*. San Francisco, CA: Jossey-Bass.

contributes to the uniqueness of a service innovation. The center part of the figure contains a symbol that we refer to as basic supply, which represents a very important category in this context. It is a category of services offered by a company and its competitors that customers also expect them to offer. Any reduction in the basic supply potentially leads to a rapid loss of customers.

Summary and Further Reading

It is important for organizations to develop a service innovation process. Many companies are not sure of how to implement such processes as they lack experience and, most of all, the tools needed to successfully adopt service innovation. Sometimes, service innovation is equated with new product development of goods, which unfortunately steers thoughts in the wrong direction in many instances.

This chapter presents our view of service innovation as new value-creating processes and customer solutions, as opposed to independent and intangible services. This means that the service can consist of a combination of direct and indirect services (a physical product), which facilitate everyday life and lead to a good experience. Service innovation refers to new value-creation processes, and understanding customer needs is a prerequisite for success.

Companies striving to increase service innovation have to establish a service development process in their organization. Such processes need not be particularly complex. Rather, they most often involve a change in thought processes. We suggest three simple phases of service innovation: finding a focus, understanding the customers in their own context, and building a solution that fits in with the rest of the organization. Adoption within the organization is often the most difficult and time-consuming phase since the service innovation has to unite new customer needs while remaining compatible with the company's existing activities. The development and implementation time for service innovation is equal to that of product innovation, although the distribution of time is completely different—the implementation time in service innovation is greater due to the number of actors involved.

Questions for the service innovator:

- Which customers or users have been involved in a recent service innovation?
- Which users should you involve in a future innovation?
- Do you have a standard service innovation process?
- What are the most important phases in your service innovation process? Does everyone agree?
- How should ideas that are conceived during the service innovation process be evaluated?
- Are you able to test service innovation and experiment in real environments?

The main sources of inspiration for this chapter are:
This chapter was inspired by the following sources:

Berry, L.L. 1999. *Discovering the Soul of Service: The Nine Drivers of Sustainable Business Success*. New York: The Free Press.

Fang, E.R., W. Palmatier, and J.B.E.M. Steenkamp. 2008. "Effect of Service Transition Strategies on Firm Value." *Journal of Marketing* 72, no. 5, pp. 1–14.

Gustafsson, A., and M.D. Johnson. 2003. *Competing in a Service Economy: How to Create a Competitive Advantage through Service Development and Innovation*. San Francisco, CA: Jossey-Bass.

Kowalkowski, C., L. Witell, and A. Gustafsson. January 2013. "Any Way Goes: Identifying Value Constellations for Service Infusion in SMEs." *Industrial Marketing Management* 42, pp. 18–30.

Prahalad, C.K., and V. Ramaswamy. 2003. "The New Frontier of Experience Innovation." *MIT Sloan Management Review* 44, no. 4, p. 12.

Witell, L., A. Gustafsson, and M.D. Johnson. 2014. "The Effect of Customer Information During New Product Development on Profits from Goods and Services." *European Journal of Marketing* 48, no. 9–10, pp. 1709–30.

CHAPTER 5

Customers as Cocreators in Service Innovation

The more you engage with customers, the clearer things become and the easier it is to determine what you should be doing.
— John Russell, Chairman of Harley Davidson

... the role of the customer is essentially that of a respondent: speaking only when spoken to.
— Eric von Hippel, Professor at MIT

This chapter covers customers taking active roles in service innovation. The most pertinent example of active customers is lead users. Lead users take matters into their own hands and innovate what they are most in need of. Lead users are identified as those who stand to most benefit from product advances, but are often identified by the fact that they are already innovating. Customer involvement encompasses how companies may identify and cooperate with those customers who possess a potential for innovation. We also discuss ethnography, a user research method used to understand the customer's value-creation processes in depth.

Preview of Action Questions

- What opportunities do your customers have to participate in your organization's service innovation process? If motivated users are engaged in your organization's innovation process, how would you benefit from that?
- Who are the lead users—the creative users who have the most to gain from innovation—if you innovate the service they already have ideas for?

- Are you experimenting with new features or models of your services?

Who Has the Most Innovative Ideas?

Imagine the following scenario: The manager at a large corporation that offers services based on technical solutions asks all employees in its development department to write down their best ideas for future innovations. A number of users are also invited to come up with ideas for the company's future range of innovations. More specifically, the users are asked to create ideas based on situations they experience in which they feel that a service would facilitate their value-creation processes, that is, that would enable them of achieving goals they experience are meaningful for them in their everyday private or working life. Thus, the customers are basically asked to create solutions they would personally find useful. The ideas for solutions that the customers suggest are constrained to be based on needs, challenges, and wishes that they have personally experienced. Customers are instructed to not simply brainstorm ideas—the ideas must arise from situations that they have experienced. The company wants to establish a connection between user ideas and value-creating processes in context.

The company has now collected two groups of ideas; internal development ideas from developers within the organization and development ideas submitted by customers, based on their personal experience. With this scenario at hand, what do you think is the answer to the following questions:

- Who do you think generated the most creative ideas for future service innovations: the personnel at the research and development (R&D) department or the customers? Why?
- Is the R&D-employees understanding of what the users would benefit from being aligned with customers' actual needs and wants?
- Are the R&D personnel capable of predicting what future solutions the customers will need?

- Were the customers sufficiently creative, or would it better to ask trained staff (such as R&D personnel) instead?

When researchers at Service Research Center (CTF) carried out a study of cell phone services designed in the aforementioned manner, results showed that the customers presented the most innovative ideas. Customers were more creative and their ideas generated more user value (as assessed by both R&D personnel and other customers). In sum, customers generated ideas that solved real and significant problems on their own.

In assessing all the ideas for future service innovation, the senior managers leading this study did not know which ideas were submitted by the customers or employees respectively as they were coded in an anonymous way. The ideas were also evaluated by several different parties—groups of customers and employees alike took part in the process. However, regardless of who evaluated the ideas, the result was the same: The customers' ideas were better. How is this possible?

This question is addressed throughout this chapter. Customers seldom get the chance to engage as actively as in this study. Customers are too rarely given the opportunity to participate in development processes at all. Most commonly, they get the chance to respond reactively to questions made up on beforehand, many times by giving ranks on a couple of items in a survey or by sitting in and talking in a focus group. We believe that customers must be given tools to facilitate service innovation involvement. Companies must use the right user facilitation method in the right situation. If these methods are not used, acquired user information may be based solely on limited memories and recollections of existing products. As noted in Chapter 3, incomplete information from customers and users unable to visualize a new service often leads to service innovation failures.

How Are Customers Involved?

Companies sometimes claim that their customers already are involved in their innovation processes. But what do their customers and users actually do? As previously mentioned, customers may be asked to give their thoughts on an existing offering used during the last six months or to voice their opinions on an almost fully operational prototype. Another common operation is to send long satisfaction surveys to customers, which typically results in low response rates. These approaches are still useful to some extent but are radically different from the knowledge your organization can collect when letting users act as a source of inspiration or as partners in development processes. Customers or users are often asked about aesthetics, design, and pricing. This means that they may be included too late in the process and asked to provide information that is not significantly related to their value creation, which should be the main goal of the innovation process. It can be said, somewhat in jest, that such customer participation encompasses decisions on what color the offering should have, or the design of the subsequent sales campaign. Again, this might be useful information for an upcoming launch, but does not include detailed problem-solving information about customer value-creation processes.

When users participate from the start in an innovation process, suggesting what should be developed and why it is important, they provide deep user information and knowledge. Usability of the service or the problem-solving capability of the offering is vital to be successful. True customer and user involvement can also give insight on how the core activities of the service should be designed, all this with the intention of innovating a service that will lead to value-cocreating processes for the customer.

In accordance with the service innovation model presented in Chapter 4, we urge everyone involved in service innovation to spend time with their customers in the customers' environment, observing and engaging them during the value-creating processes. Ensure that users are equipped with an appropriate set of "tools" to modify and test the service or physical product as it will increase the likelihood that submitted ideas are useful. This set of tools depends on what the service innovation process encompasses—in, for instance, telecommunication services, a mobile phone is a good tool to let customers more easily share their thoughts on future mobile services. A mobile phone allows customers to take pictures, register their thoughts and experiences, and submit them to the company. In health care facilities, where mobile phones are not always allowed, the act of blogging or writing a diary covering one's experiences has shown to be a successful platform. By providing the customers with the enabling tools, the sharing of information about value creation will be facilitated.

Another example of tool use can be found in the travel industry, where select customers of a travel firm are encouraged to send a text message every time something extraordinary happens. Text messages can also be sent to a target customer group at different times to inquire about how they are occupied, to get information about value creating opportunities (and challenges). Academically procedures such as these are referred to as "experience sampling".

Selecting which customers should participate in the service innovation process is very important. Our research, and that of others as well, shows that motivated participants should always be at the forefront. Selection should not involve identifying any kind of average customer or employment of random selection procedure.

Early Involvement

Research articles show increased likelihood of success when letting users participate in early stages of the innovation process. Although it is always beneficial to listen to customers, the value of customer input can be significantly enhanced by involving them as early as possible in the development process, which is in contrast to current industry practice. For service innovation, it is also important to not forget to involve customers also later in the development process when there exists a description or prototype of the service. This allows for smoother adoption processes. Too many potential innovations never get a chance as companies have not considered how customers will adopt the new service.

Early involvement to some extent requires different techniques than late development input. With inspiration from research on information systems we have created a descriptive model aimed at elucidating this issue to companies by covering the manner in which they listen to customers, as six stages of customer or user involvement:

1. We do not listen to customers. New products originate from new technology and competence.

2. We do not listen to customers. However, we base our product development on our perception and estimates of customer needs.

3. We listen to customers via questionnaires, interviews, or focus groups but do not involve them in our development processes.

4. Customers are involved in the development process by testing new products (e.g., in user-labs) and giving feedback.

5. Customers are actively involved in the development process and allowed to submit their own ideas.

6. The customers develop products for themselves since there are no value creating solutions available on the market.

We note that several companies seldom reach past stage 3 of this model, which represents the traditional market survey or reactive methods (interviews, focus groups, and questionnaires) mentioned in Chapter 3. Stages 4 to 6 are markedly different from the first three stages; they entail far greater customer involvement in the innovation process. In the last two stages (5 and 6), customers are in fact the most active party as they carry out the bulk of the innovation process themselves. Stage 6 represents Lead Users who develop innovations for themselves when no market solutions that meet their needs exist.

Lead Users

The notion that all new products or services originate from companies is a commonly held belief. When a product or service, old or new, is used and found to be lacking in some way, statements such as "it's strange that they (the company) don't do anything to fix this" are common. The belief that companies invariably sow all seeds of innovation seem well rooted in the human mind. However, to budge this belief just a little bit, consider how skilled we humans are at adapting to new situations— our problem-solving skills peak whenever a crucial situation occurs. Also, people are in general both more well-educated and can obtain new knowledge much faster today than, let's say, 25 years ago. In the innovation history, users have proven to be the source to ideas for, for example, rollerblades, the coffee filter, and the Frisbee. Our point is that it is not strange that customers are good at finding solutions, even if it is not part of their day job. What is strange is that we have the view of companies as the originators of innovation, such a belief is narrow minded and research suggest that we should adjust our view of innovators to also incorporate the customer or user.

Figure 5.1 illustrates a modern irrigation system used on large arable land areas. It is referred to as a "center pivot irrigation system" in technical terminology. This innovation is absolutely extraordinary as it enables irrigation of vast areas of land in a cost- and energy-efficient manner. An irrigation system such as this is obviously available on the market via various industrial companies that most likely manufacture, sell, and offer ancillary maintenance services as well. The development trends of this type of large industrial irrigation systems have followed the innovation logic previously presented, that is, they have been developed by different companies in a number of iterations, eventually becoming the modern and indispensable service for farmers shown in Figure 5.1. Center pivot irrigation systems have proven to be very useful, allowing farmers to grow crops in desert environments where water is a scarce resource. This service innovation has provided value of significant importance to social development.

Figure 5.1 A modern irrigation system based on the center pivot principle

Source: www.valleyirrigation.com/valley-irrigation/us/mediaroom/photos#centerpivots

The interesting aspect of the center pivot irrigation system is that it did not originate from the manufacturers that today build them, but instead from a lead user who was facing a problem and had a strong need to solve it. Note that even for a complex industrial business-to-business offering, a user was the creative source behind the innovation. Frank Zybach is an American farmer who was not satisfied with the harvest produced on his farm. He had a strong desire to develop an irrigation system that would enable him to run his farm more productively. How was it possible for an ordinary farmer to develop such an important innovation in an established industry that was serviced by world-class corporations?

The secret behind Frank Zybach's innovation (see Figure 5.2) was that he had (1) a very strong need for large-scale irrigation, (2) a history that had given him an aptitude for problem solving, and (3) the tools to fashion a working system based on his ideas. A strong need, which involves intrinsic motivation, connected to knowledge and the tools to create a solution is, as shown by research, a winning formula for innovation.

Frank Zybach grew up on the countryside and encountered the problems of poor irrigation firsthand at an early age. Frank's father was a smith and taught him how to develop water management systems based on the pressure that develops when water is led through interconnected

Figure 5.2 Frank Zybach's own irrigation system
Source: www.livinghistoryfarm.org

steel pipes. As such, Frank had the tools required to solve the problem at hand. These skills, coupled with the strong needs he had of improving as a farmer, led to his successful innovation. The irrigation system he developed also contained several interesting details but the concept of interconnecting pipes to power the rotation around its own axle was the most important one. Water fed from the pivot point in the center is then distributed into long pipes. This resulted in the ability to irrigate numerous crop circles and revolutionized the entire agricultural landscape of the United States. It was later picked up by several companies that further developed the system and distributed it to the rest of the world.

A similar example, described in his research around Lead Users by MIT-professor Eric von Hippel in a Sloan Management Review interview,[1] is the invention of the heart–lung bypass machine by Dr. Heysham Gibbon. Dr. Gibbon was frustrated by a lack of product offerings from the medical device companies to help patients dying from circulatory problems. So he developed the bypass machine himself. Furthermore, one of the authors of this book worked in the financial trading business when most financial securities and derivatives trading moved online: He observed that most of the innovations in how orders entered online originated from active traders who were trying to get an edge over competitors. A final example of user innovation is the phenomenon of open source software, which includes major "brands" such as Apache and Linux, and is totally reliant on innovation from users.

Despite the fact that key innovations in agricultural irrigation, medical devices, online trading, and countless other services and physical products came from users with a strong desire who were capable of solving the problem at hand, most companies still seem stuck in the belief that their development teams or R&D centers are the sole originators of innovations. This belief is in contrast to how to the key reasons why Lead Users, outside the firm, develop innovations that provide value for themselves. Again, the key to these innovations was a strong need for the innovation from users who, from experience and occupation, have developed

---

[1] von Hippel, E. 2011. "The User Innovation Revolution." *MIT Sloan Management Review*, September 21. http://sloanreview.mit.edu/article/the-user-innovation-revolution/

skills and insight into possible solutions. Coupled with motivation that stems from a strong need this makes a perfect ground for service innovation. This represents a completely different mode of operation for service innovation.

Why do so many people stubbornly cling to the notion that only companies should develop innovations? Perhaps, the cases of Frank Zybach, Dr. Gibbon, the online traders, open source software users, and the many other examples available are really only "exceptions proving the rule" that new products and services should indeed be developed by companies without any customer involvement? However, studies by American innovation researcher Eric von Hippel have actually shown that this is not true (see Table 5.1).

Many users try to improve products and services. According to one avenue of research, at least 6 percent of the users generally make adjustment to their purchased offerings that could be labeled innovations. The numbers in Table 5.1 are based on explainable logic pointing to the fact that surgeons probably care a lot about their work and that they are very much interested in any measure capable of facilitating or improving the result of their work. The same principle applies to mountain bike cyclists—regardless of being regular enthusiasts or bona fide professionals,

Table 5.1 The number of innovations created by users in different markets

Products	Sample	Percentage of innovations developed for personal use
CAD software circuit boards	136 participants at a CAD conference	24.3
Library information systems	Librarians at 102 libraries in Australia	26.0
Surgical equipment	261 surgeons at surgical clinics in Germany	22.0
Extreme sport equipment (e.g., skydiving)	197 members of various clubs that organize extreme sports	37.8
Mountain bike equipment	291 mountain bikers in a particular region	19.2

Source: von Hippel, E. 2005. Democratizing Innovation. Cambridge, MA: MIT Press.

they use their bicycles to a great degree and have thereby acquired experience and knowledge that can be used to further develop their bicycles in different aspects. Whether it be irrigation systems, medical devices, trading screens, software, mobile phones, pellet burners, hotel stays, or broadband services, customers have identified problems and performed or suggested innovations to solve the problems. The key is combining the experiences from users with problem-solving skills and a strong motivation. Add tools for innovation to that and invited customers will be able of contributing to the innovation processes of any company within any industry.

Astute readers might notice that the majority of innovation examples cited by Dr. Eric von Hippel involved lead users and physical products. Research also shows the value of lead users in the innovation of traditional (direct) services. One research study carried out in the banking sector, also by von Hippel, showed that nearly 40 services had been developed by regular users and subsequently developed further by bank. These new services were mainly in security and online banking. Online trading and open source software examples were already cited in this discussion. The service company called Weight Watchers was started by Jean Nidetch, who was unhappy with her weight and unable to find solutions that she found satisfying to help her. She started her own club consisting of female friends who supported each other, and the result is the commercial weight loss program that is top rated by *US News*. Again, skills with how to tailor-make a solution coupled with a strong need makes a fertile ground for service innovation.

User innovation is natural for products viewed as services: One of the key tenets of service marketing—a part of the definition of service—is the cocreation of value by users and producers.[2] Companies that view themselves as service providers are therefore familiar with the cocreation of value concept. Logically, a focus on and understanding of the value-creation process and implementing user innovation should be easier under a service paradigm due to this acknowledgment of the cocreation of value.

---

[2] Bitner, M., W.T. Faranda, A.R. Hubbert, and V.A. Zeithaml. 1997. "Customer Contributions and Roles in Service Delivery." *International Journal of Service Industry Management* 8, no. 3, pp. 193–205.

Eric von Hippel's research into lead users has received increasing amount of attention in recent years. The research team of von Hippel's at MIT in Boston decided to examine what the potential of lead users consisted of compared to ideas developed internally. Table 5.2 shows the result of this experiment. The comparison between the two different principles that are based on creating ideas internally and identifying them as lead users, respectively, shows that there is great potential for innovation processes that are carried out in an outward–inward paradigm. Lead users who are aligned with their context simply generate better ideas. Include customers in the service innovation processes, especially your lead users. Their ideas are more innovative and profitable.

In the study of cell phone service that started the chapter, customers were found to have more original value creating ideas not because users are inherently more creative than R&D staff—rather, customers have unique knowledge of situations of value-creating processes important to them, as well as important details of their situations and environment. They have knowledge and skills about the use of the solution while the employees within a firm have knowledge and skills about the solution. If these two entities of knowledge can be connected innovation processes will run a lot smoother. The solution most often utilizes resources the company has access to and knowledge of. The need often arises in situations in which the user has skills and knowledge. While the company

Table 5.2 Comparison between innovation ideas created internally and those that originate from lead users

	Lead user ideas	Product development ideas
Creativity (scale 1–10)	9.6	6.8
As yet unknown customer values (scale 1–10)	8.3	5.3
Market share after five years	68%	33%
Sales after five years	US$146	US$18
Success probability	80%	66%

Source: Lilien, G.L., P.D. Morrison, K. Searls, M. Sonnack, and E. von Hippel. 2002. "Performance Assessment of the Lead User Idea-Generation Process for New Product Development." *Management Science* 48, no. 8, pp. 1042–59.

most likely possesses the most knowledge of the process and technology of a solution, the customers are in closest proximity to their own needs.

Users are simply more knowledgeable of their own reality or value-creation processes than the R&D developers employed on behalf of the companies. Imagine a situation in which a 40-year-old, well-paid, professional, male engineer is tasked with finding solutions that appeal to an unemployed teenage girl who has grown up without exposure to information technology solutions. It goes without saying that it would be very difficult for the engineer to identify with her needs as well as her situation and environment where the need is present. Contextual aspects far removed from our own context and needs are simply more difficult to envision. One example proving this fact is when packing clothes for a holiday far away in the sun on a cold winter morning, you have most likely packed one sweater or a pair of trousers too many simply because it is appropriate in your current situation.

The telephone communication company that we studied would hardly have been able to understand—even with expensive and extensive customer surveys—the venue and details of all their customers' value-creating processes. It is unlikely that questions in in-depth interviews or user focus groups would be enough to identify the situations that occurred in their customers' everyday life. When we subsequently allowed the customers to experience and base their feedback on situations that were important to them, and that occurred in their everyday life, a number of ideas arose that were based on situations that the company, even with a good portion of creativity, would not have been able to think of beforehand. All customer ideas were based on situations the customers had in fact experienced, which is the reason why they were regarded as creative and value creating. The ideas of companies are often instead based on existing and available technology, that is, they are developed in accordance with a paradigm, or logic, that we earlier (in Chapter 1) classified as inside-out. Our follow-up interviews with both customers and employees also showed that the customers based their solutions on rather ordinary, but still for the customer important, situations, while the employees relied on technical solutions they found interesting.

One random and interesting discovery we made in the study was that, when confronted, most customers, especially those who had suggested the ideas the researchers who assessed the merit of the ideas had identified as very creative, were surprised by the high ranking of their ideas. These innovative customers said something similar to: "I just based my solution on a situation I encountered once when I was downtown." Thus, they were ordinary for the customer but gave creative insights to the developers within the company.

In research terms, customer involvement in service development is important because it is often carried out on site, which means that companies have tried to create important components of the service innovation specifically where it is thought to have a subsequent effect. In contrast, customer and user surveys that are carried out outside the context of use, for instance, in conference rooms, far removed from where the service is going to be used in the future, are less likely to provide an organization with much help into the innovation process. For finding service innovations, we recommend that the company leave the conference room and go wherever the value-creation processes occur. This applies to everyone except companies that sell conference room equipment!

A survey attempting to analyze, for instance, customer opinions on a number of gardening tools is best carried out during a pleasant spring day in the beginning of May when people are most likely to be working in their gardens, as opposed to using telephone interviews on an ice cold winter day. Similarly, it is difficult to get patient opinions on hospital stays after they have left the hospital and have perhaps already recovered. The experience will not be the same as when the patients were actually at the hospital with an illness. Most likely everyone who has stayed at a hotel have received, three to four days subsequent to the visit, a request to fill out a short satisfaction survey. Unfortunately, surveys as these will give the hotel manager very little information about how to improve the service of the hotel. If a hotel manager really would like to understand how to improve a hotel, they would do much better hanging around in the reception area talking and observing customers when they arrive and leave the hotel.

As shown in Table 5.3, there is an important difference between the previously mentioned lead-user studies and those in which customers are allowed to provide solution proposals based on situations they have

Table 5.3 *Lead user methodology compared to customer involvement*

Lead user methodology	Customer involvement
The users identify a strong need, which, if solved, would lead to value-creation processes. They create the solution to the problem on their own as there is no existing market solutions available.	Users identify problems in the value-creation processes but do not create any solutions, only ideas for solutions, or prototypes for how a solution that they would experience valuable could function. An organization is working in partnership with the customer or user.

personally experienced, as in the telephone company example. We refer to the latter as customer involvement. The essence of the lead-user method is that the users themselves both identify value-creating processes and create a solution to them, this is totally without any interaction of a company (the lead users engage in innovation because there are no solutions provided on a market). In our study, customers identified value-creating processes and suggested relevant ideas. However, they never created or realized a complete solution. Most companies do not need to go as far as a complete solution since they can instead let the customers identify value-creating processes and potential solutions from which subsequent solutions are developed. In light of Chapter 4, this means that we involve customers in the understanding of the process, and the goal of the company can still be to identify and implement possible solutions.

We have participated in customer involvement projects in health care. In one of our studies, patients were provided with idea books in which they could write down how they experienced their illness when they experienced it. They were asked to describe the situation when the illness arose, and how they dealt with it. Those in charge of developing health care were given access to the patient ideas and could use that as important feedback of how the patients felt about their care and how the provided care contributed to the patients improvement of health. The project provided the health care staff with knowledge of problems experienced by the patients in their homes or when they were transferred between different parts of the health care institution, that is, essential aspects of the patients' value-creation processes. Patients with chronic diseases in particular, such as cancer or chronic pain, are experts of their disease and know how to handle it on a daily basis. Some examples of the problems patients experienced was the difficulty of seeing what time it is at night when lying on one's back without being able to move, how seriously a disease affects one's ability to cope with three children as a single parent, or how to handle the sometimes contradictory advice given at different departments in the health care institution. These types of situations are typically not what health-care employees (i.e. nurses and doctors) are informed or know much about, nevertheless, it affects the value that the patient will experience from health-care service.

One of the authors worked for an online trading software company that provided free rent to an active online trading firm so that first-tier traders would be located just one floor below the company's development staff. Engineers and product development managers observed their firm's products in use and gathered live feedback from demanding cutting-edge (lead) users. The company found that the insight gained from value creation observation and real-time discussion was worth far more than the rent and software license subsidy granted to the trading firm. Fortunately, such subsidies are rarely needed: Users are often very pleased, even honored, to participate in service innovation without any subsidy.

Understanding Customer Contexts—Ethnographic Studies

Moving from a discussion of user innovation and user involvement we are now to discuss an intensive user research method, namely the ethnographic research method. We mentioned an ethnographic study of customers in Chapter 3 along with other user research techniques, but felt that more complete discussion of ethnographic techniques is motivated.

Service innovation relies heavily on understanding user needs and situations or contexts, as established in Chapter 4. Successful service innovation is always based on an understanding and enhancement of the value-creating processes of the user. Only after understanding the value-creation process and associated problems should the company be able of determine what resources are needed in order to realize the innovation of a new value proposition (see Chapter 4). In traditional innovation processes, companies often do the exact opposite: They begin by researching and developing an offering they believe is profitable or attractive and *then* examine how it might be useful to customers. Analyzing the situation from a broader perspective we suggest that the customer's context represents the lifeblood in service development, while the company's laboratories represent the lifeblood in traditional product development.

One problem with the development-first, then understanding, innovation processes is that the company risks incurring great development costs that might not be justifiable in relation to profits of future sales, unless it manages to persuade the customer to purchase the offer despite not being a perfect match.

Ethnography is a tool borrowed from anthropology based on holistic logic stipulating that aspects of an entity or process cannot be understood or analyzed independently. Ethnographical studies often follow users during the activities in which value is generated. As a result, the context where value is being created is naturally integrated in ethnographic research.

A study of the Scandinavian airline, SAS, examined air travelers' perceptions of their trip by filming and interviewing them in situ while at the airport, at check-in, on-board, and at the baggage claim, following them until reaching their final destination. SAS also had travelers write diaries during these different stages where they detailed elements of pleasure and annoyance. It is easier to acquire insight and understand value-creating processes if the travelers in question are in the particular situation where value creation occurs, as opposed to asking them after a period of time to provide a recollection from memory (as was also pointed out in the hotel example a couple of pages ago). Research has shown that many recollections of well-being and irritation fade quickly.

There are many other examples of useful marketing insights from ethnographic research. Nike has sent anthropologists to inner-city playgrounds to watch urban youth, who have been leading fashion setters for sport footwear, use and wear expensive shoes. On some occasions, a truck load of shoes were left to see which colors and styles were taken and which were later worn on the basketball courts. An academic researcher, trying to understand how high-tech firms performed marketing, gained insight from observing a tech firm working for several months.

An interesting (and strange) example of insight into a value-creation process from in-depth qualitative research was the case of new home insecticides for roaches. A target pool of low-income southern women agreed that products that were test marketed—plastic trays that killed roaches discretely—worked better and were less messy than roach sprays. But they continued to buy the sprays. After interviews, observation, and other qualitative research, the marketing team determined that these customers viewed cockroaches as symbols of the men in their lives. "Killing the roaches with a bug spray and watching them squirm and die allowed the women to express their hostility toward men and have greater control ...."[3] This would have never been a question on a survey. No one at the company was likely to guess that there was a positive user experience from watching the roaches after they were sprayed!

A more mainstream example of the power of ethnographic study is studies of mobile phone use in developing countries. When mobile phone use was still relatively new, several mobile phone companies sent ethnographic teams into China, India, and other developing countries to observe how the phones were being used in remote villages that had new mobile service. They found that due to high cost but corresponding high value created, extended families and even whole villages were finding ways to share cell phone service. The findings from the studies led to the development of low-cost Internet phones and special service bundles suited for the observed phone sharing.

Ethnographical research breaks many of the traditions used as guidelines in classical market research. For instance, ethnography does not rely on random selection of different subjects, but instead attempts to identify users capable of making extraordinary contributions. The approach is similar, but not identical, to identifying lead users. These rich subjects can then be used to find additional subjects. Ethnography relies on close collaboration between said users and their personal experiences that leads to insight and understanding of the situations that either facilitate or obstruct value-creation processes. Understanding how people live makes it possible to discover otherwise elusive trends that can provide companies with future strategic leads.

---

[3] Alsop, R. 1988. "Advertisers Put Consumers on the Couch." *Wall Street Journal,* May 13.

Take smartphones as an example: Ethnography can identify differences between technologically savvy teenagers who have been using mobile phones since first grade and older generations of people who grew up when mobile phones did not even exist. Ethnographical studies aid in transferring the perspective of a consumer group to employees at a company. It is worth noting that the electronics company Intel has some 24 ethnographically trained persons in its staff.

Let us examine the previously mentioned study of SAS in more detail. Through several ethnographical studies, a significantly clearer picture of air travelers' real needs developed. Having originally focused on safety and pricing as the customers' central needs, SAS was able, through the studies, to identify other processes through which it could support customers via a cohesive traveling process and thereby develop their brand while maintaining relatively high price levels.

Figure 5.3 shows a hierarchy of experiences in which air travelers have rated the priority of value-creation processes. The first stages in the figure

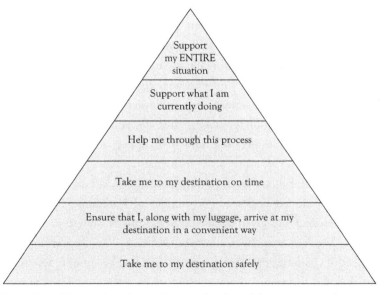

Figure 5.3 Hierarchy of experiences developed from air travelers via ethnographical methods[4]

---

[4] Ekdahl, F., A. Gustafsson, and B. Edvardsson. 1999. "Customer-oriented Service Development at SAS." *Managing Service Quality: An International Journal* 9, no. 6, pp. 403–410.

contain essential elements such as safety, baggage handling, and timeliness. When the airline is able to meet the requirements that transport the traveler safely from point A to B, it can advance upward through the pyramidal hierarchy. In order to compete with other companies, subsequent amenities might consist of providing travelers with the opportunity to work when traveling, which includes everything including Wi-Fi, workspace, and the ability to speak uninterrupted on the phone. However, this also includes resources that assist passengers when traveling to and from the airport. One example of supporting the traveler's entire situation (the topmost section of the pyramid) is awarding loyalty points that can be used to rent cars or pay for hotel stays. Providing support in this way is a prime example of service logic: The company supports a user and his or her value-creation processes.

Many innovations involve new technology that has not always been developed with the customers' value-creating processes in mind, but rather because it has been technically possible. Service innovations that support value-creation processes can obviously, in many cases, consist of new technology, but they are often accompanied by different types of activities on behalf of frontline staff as well. These activities in particular, as noted in Chapter 4, are difficult to copy, ranging from the slightest contact between employee and customer to large chains of interlinked activities in the form of actions that employees carry out to support the customer's value-creation processes. This domain makes it possible to speak in terms of complete solutions that support what customers want to do.

Frontline staff plays an important part in ethnographical studies. In the aforementioned SAS study, a number of interesting findings were made when staff was given detailed descriptions of how to carry out the studies. The first was the realization that they actually encountered a number of customer problems every day but had become so desensitized that they did not regard them as problems or even considered measures to eliminate them permanently by targeting the root cause. Instead, they solved every specific situation ad hoc. The second finding was that customers were highly adaptive and did not regard said problems as customer problems either. Therefore, they were not able to recognize or remember all sources of annoyance when queried by the staff, in effect also undergoing a process of desensitization in which problems were taken for granted.

The ethnographical studies made it possible for SAS to discover needs that were not explicitly stated but important nonetheless. SAS also discovered that customers had created minor workaround routines, which encompassed everything from putting up Post-it notes with the ticket number on the bag to finding ways of cramming the luggage into the overhead bin, as well as finding positions in the airplane seat that were suitable when sleeping. Via ethnographical survey methods, the staff eventually discovered and came to understand all of these small impediments, which enabled the company to develop solutions that not only eliminated sources of annoyance but also facilitated and improved the customers' overall traveling experience.

Facilitate Customer Cocreation of Service Innovation

Customers are becoming increasingly involved in the service innovation processes in organizations. Compare what it was like to enter a retail establishment 50 years ago with the condition today. Customers now walk around the store collecting products, placing them in their shopping bag, and often making the payment without any interaction with staff. The same phenomenon is observed at gas stations, airports, banks, and so on, and the overall trend is moving toward a situation in which customers are taking care of the processes themselves. Self-service is another challenge and opportunity for service innovation. It is important for organizations to ask themselves what kinds of processes they can let their customers carry out themselves, with better results for their value-creating process as a promising goal. Interestingly, vice versa is also true, organizations can also ask themselves what processes the customers already are doing, and see if they can innovate something that enables them to do it instead (again, if enhanced value-creating processes occur for the customer).

What are the key factors that facilitate customer involvement, whether during the actual moment of consumption or during the stages of the development process? Research suggests six factors that facilitate involvement from customers as cocreators in service innovation processes.[5] The odds of customer involvement in service innovation processes improve if:

- They have expertise. All service innovation processes that encompass areas such as exercise, hobbies, cars, renovations, or do-it-yourself (DIY) activities are facilitated if the customers have expertise. Think of the examples of the farmers, doctors, and traders in our discussion of user creation.
- They wish to be in control. Service innovation processes that encompass offers in which the customer or user wishes to be in control of the results always facilitate cocreation. Customer desire for more control over their personal finances has been a major factor in online banking development.
- Physical capital is available. Service innovation processes that require physical capital are obviously facilitated by the fact that the requisite tools, space, or other resources are available to certain customers. For instance, in software development, customers must install certain software before participating in service innovation processes.
- They wish to minimize risks. Service innovation processes are facilitated when customers are strong proponents of risk minimization. Patient participation in health care innovation is more likely if it results in a lowered risk of becoming ill or experiencing negative consequences from a disease.
- Their involvement leads to experiences. One of the primary reasons why customers participate in service innovation processes is that they find them enjoyable and that the act of creating creates value. For instance, many web-based companies encourage customers to submit ideas of new foods, traveling services, or home-improvement projects.
- The innovations lead to financial or need-related benefits. One of the deciding factors of customer participation in

service innovation processes is whether or not it results in saving time and money. It can involve making improvement suggestions to the organization or providing ideas of how to develop a time-saving service. For instance, the motivation for railway customers to participate in service innovation is often that it will result in benefits to them, for example, a more reliable trip.

The aforementioned factors not only elucidate dimensions that facilitate customer participation in service innovation processes, but also the extent to which they will participate. The trend of motivated customers who want to participate in service innovation processes should lead companies away from the traditional mindset of "what can I do for you?" to an environment where customers are instead asked "what can we do together?"

Summary and Further Reading

The philosophy of this book is that the customer belongs in the driver's seat to promote development of new offerings tailored to their own value-creating processes. Your challenge as a service innovator is to determine how to establish a functional process that enhances the development of customer value creation. This requires a conscious effort on your part to activate your customers and equip them with the necessary knowledge and tools to ensure that they successfully negotiate the challenge at hand. Perhaps hardest of all: You must be willing to actually place customers in the driver's seat and learn both from them and with them. It is more easily said than done as research confirms that open and collaborative innovation processes are perceived as unfamiliar and difficult by most companies. However, this chapter has provided you with some important insights into the process of involving the customer into the development and is based on knowledge that we have had the privilege to apply on a number of companies, including Ericsson, TeliaSonera, Whirlpool, Public organizations, and a leading French bank.

Involve customers and users in service innovation. The result will be new services that better enables customer value creation. Our research indicates another side benefit: Customers involved in the innovation process are likely to become even more loyal customers and become evangelists for the new service if they are allowed to influence the development in their own desired direction.

Questions for the service innovator:

- What opportunities do your customers have to participate in your organization's development process?
- Who are the lead users of your current services?
- What sources does your organization use to generate ideas of future innovations?
- Have other sources for ideas been investigated sufficiently?
- Do you continue customer testing and research during the launch of a new service? Development?
- Do you offer services that would benefit and evolve from continual A/B testing?

The main sources of inspiration for this chapter are:

The empirical studies where users proved to be better idea generators than company employees, is well documented in the following articles:

Kristensson, P., P. Magnusson, and J. Matthing. 2002. "Users as a Hidden Resource for Creativity: Findings from an Experimental Study on User Involvement." *Creativity and Innovation Management* 11, no. 1, pp. 55–61.

Kristensson, P., A. Gustafsson, and T. Archer. 2004. "Harnessing the Creative Potential Among Users." *Journal of Product Innovation Management* 21, no. 1, pp. 4–14.

Magnusson, P., J. Matthing, and P. Kristensson. 2003. "Managing User Involvement in Service Innovation: Experiments with Innovating End Users." *Journal of Service Research* 6, no. 2, pp. 111–24.

Magnusson, P.R. 2009. "Exploring the Contributions of Involving Ordinary Users in Ideation of Technology-Based Services." *Journal of Product Innovation Management* 26, no. 5, pp. 578–93.

We have also compared different data collection models to examine the efficacy of in-depth interviews and focus groups in relation to a more interactive milieu in which customers are activated in their own context. Said studies are documented in:

> Kristensson, P., J. Matthing, and N. Johansson. 2008. "Key Strategies in Co-Creation of New Services." *Journal of Service Management* 19, no. 4, pp. 474–91.
>
> Witell, L., P. Kristensson, A. Gustafsson, and M. Löfgren. 2011. "Idea Generation: Customer Co-Creation Versus Traditional Market Research Techniques." *Journal of Service Management* 22, no. 2, pp. 140–59.

This chapter is also based on additional ideas and concepts with regard to service development and service innovation. Some of the examples used are more elaborately described in the following sources:

> Edvardsson, B., A. Gustafsson, M.D. Johnson, and B. Sandén. 2000. *New Service Development in the New Economy.* Lund, Sweden: Studentlitteratur.
>
> Elg, M., J. Engström, L. Witell, and B. Poksinska. 2012. "Co-Creation and Learning in Health-Care Service Development." *Journal of Service Management* 23, no. 3, pp. 328–43.
>
> Schirr, G.R. 2012. "User Research for Product Innovation." In *The PDMA Handbook of New Product Development,* eds. K.B. Kahn, S.E. Kay, R.J. Slotegraaf, and S. Uban. Hoboken, NJ: John Wiley & Sons, Inc. doi: 10.1002/9781118466421.ch14

A plethora of well-written articles and books exists on the subject of Eric von Hippel's groundbreaking research. We have chosen to highlight five pieces here. The first one is a comparison of financial data that lead users generate for companies and the second one encompasses lead users within service companies. The third one in the following row is one of the first articles on this theme and the fourth is a book summarizing the research area. The last one is a shorter article of the same theme. More information about examples and business cases can be found on his website at MIT or at www.leaduser.com.

Lilien, G.L., P.D. Morrison, K. Searls, M. Sonnack, and E. von Hippel. 2002. "Performance Assessment of the Lead User Idea-Generation Process for New Product Development." *Management Science* 48, no. 8, pp. 1042–59.

Oliveira, P., and E. von Hippel. 2011. "Users as Service Innovators: The Case of Banking Services." *Research Policy* 40, no. 6, pp. 806–18.

von Hippel, E. 1978. "Successful Industrial Products from Customer Ideas." *Journal of Marketing* 42, no. 1, pp. 39–49.

von Hippel, E. 2005. *Democratizing Innovation*. Cambridge, MA: MIT Press.

von Hippel, E., S. Thomke, and M. Sonnack. 1999. "Creating Breakthroughs at 3M." *Harvard Business Review* 77, no. 5, pp. 47–57.

If the reader would like to further explore ideas in market validation, we recommend the footnotes in the list of the five processes, especially Brown on Design Thinking and Ries and Bland on Lean Innovation.

CHAPTER 6

Service Innovation in Goods-Centric Firms

Get closer than ever to your customer. So close in fact, that you tell them what they need well before they realize it themselves.

—Steve Jobs, founder of Apple

A business absolutely devoted to service will have only one worry about profits: They will be embarrassingly large.

—Henry Ford

This chapter covers the final topic of this book, service innovation in firms with a goods-centric mindset. This topic obviously applies to traditional goods manufacturers who realize that their customers value service. However, even some traditional service organizations view their standardized services like goods and can be considered goods-centric. In health care, goods-centricity is often used to produce care as efficient and profitable as possible. We briefly discuss why and how these "goods-centric" or "product focused" firms try to increase the share of services and how they use service innovation to differentiate their offerings. We also discuss various service strategies and how firms can change their business models to start charging for services that have previously been offered for free.

A consistent theme throughout this book is that by focusing on the "job" of the customer, all goods become service. Traditional goods firms have to rethink their innovation process to take advantage of this perspective. "The transition from a Goods Logic (product focus) to Service Logic (customer [or value creation] focus) is a time and resource intensive process that requires committed leadership and a significant organization-wide cultural shift."[1] We talk about the efforts such firms must undertake to be successful in this transition which we refer to as "service infusion."

Preview of Action Questions

While you are reading this chapter think about these questions, especially if you work in a manufacturer or a goods-centric firm.

- What services does your organization currently provide to its customers or users?
- Which of these services are free?
- Which of the free services *could* your firm charge for?

Goods-Centric Firms

We believe that all organizations eventually will be forced by competition to change the focus from their goods toward facilitating and improving the everyday lives of their customers. Customers do not really need goods—they need the job the goods can do for them—that is, a clean car, extra time, a hole drilled in the wall, or a transport from one place to another. We are currently witnessing a revolution in what traditional goods firms offer customers. Firms that have long focused on goods are undergoing a paradigm shift to service logic.

Goods-centric firms generally identify their offerings as products, but so do some firms in the service sector. Examples of service industries where it is common to speak in terms of "products" are banks offering "financial products" such as self-service banking, car or home loans, and credit cards, and insurance firms offering term, variable, and whole-life life insurance products. In both health care and public transport, a large emphasis is placed on measures that improve "product quality."

---

[1] Brown, S.W., A. Gustafsson, and L. Witell. 2011. "Service Logic: Transforming Product-Focused Businesses." White Paper, Center for Service Leadership. Arizona State University. https://wpcareyschool.qualtrics.com/CP/File.php?F=F_00Y8lUIfzIYxQ3P

Firms can change this focus. As an example, Petsmart has evolved from being simply a pet store stocked with a wide variety of pet-related goods to a service center focusing on helping pet owners in their everyday lives through educational programs and hotels for pets and (sometimes) also for the owners. At many locations, Petsmart offers customers the opportunity to meet and consult a veterinarian; the veterinary service is sometimes offered by annual retainer. When a goods firm views its offerings as services, it initiates a major paradigm shift. As noted, we refer to the transition from goods logic to service logic and the resulting focus on service innovation as "service infusion."

Service for Increased Competitiveness

During service infusion, value creation and service become the locus of strategy, ideally leading to greater revenue and profitability. Service differentiate a firm in a highly competitive market by focusing on the effects of the products and services on users, rather than on the technical characteristics of the products.

IBM is widely viewed as a pioneer in service infusion. Other notable industrial firms like GE, Volvo, Cisco, Ericsson, EMC, and SKF have also increased their profitability through service infusion. The focus on service infusion in traditional goods–centric Western firms is in part an effort to face the competition from Africa, India, China, and the rest of Asia. As commoditization impacts their goods, Western firms do not want to compete on price with low-cost competitors in the developing world.

Moving from a goods logic to a service logic based on solutions where a combination of physical products and services solves customers' problems poses an organizational challenge. Service innovation is a strategic way to face this challenge. As firms move from a focus on transactions toward relationships and the customers' value-creation processes, they establish a bond with their customers, making it undesirable and difficult to switch to a competitor.

When customers feel that the performance and features of products are increasingly similar, competition forces firms to either differentiate their offerings as more attractive or compete through lower prices. How large are the differences between competing offerings in, for instance, electrical supply, telephone, and airline industries? A review would most likely uncover only minor differences, making price the primary attribute that customers use to choose between the brands. In order to avoid getting locked into price wars, firms must solve the customers' problems better than the competitors.

A firm that has undergone service infusion considers goods as platforms for service provision. If, for instance, a customer purchases a truck-based transport solution, the truck itself might not be sufficient to enable a successful solution for the customer—maintenance, performance monitoring, and advisory services on driving patterns and fuel consumption are also needed. For private customers, the transport solution may consist of access to rental bicycles that are distributed at various places throughout the city as well as access to public transportation. For business customers, the transport solution may consist of leasing trucks that are serviced at regular intervals, or leasing trucks with a driver included.

The key is that the offering must meet the prerequisites for value creation. Transitioning from the role of a goods supplier to a service provider requires the organization to reevaluate its knowledge of customers, the organization's offerings, and how offerings are developed. A customer using a service does not perceive value the same way as a customer using a physical product. Increasing the service content of an offering introduces variation in the performance, in part by making the customer a part of the service. Services are more subjective than products, especially when customers actively contribute to create value in use.

A goods-centric firm aiming to differentiate through service must succeed at service infusion. The firm needs to outline a strategy and a system for developing innovative offerings that are not based on its product portfolio but on the value-creation processes of customers. A firm that is able to successfully develop both technological innovations and innovative services can create a unique offering, thus gaining a competitive advantage. However, research shows that it is challenging to combine and succeed with product and service innovation in the same organization.

Goods as a Platform for Service

American and Swedish industrial history includes many manufacturing firms whose technological innovation subsequently transformed them into global market leaders in their industries. Firms like IBM, Ericsson, GE, Volvo, Caterpillar, SKF, Cummins Engine, Tetra Pak, Apple, Electrolux, Cisco, and many others owe their success to strong technological innovations. Today, it is as important for firms to succeed in service innovation in order to offer solutions that ensure important value-creation processes for customers. This is the key to becoming a market leader.

IBM sells processing units or time, while operating the computer centers. Volvo Buses is in the business of selling "uptime" or transport system availability. Uptime refers to the time period when a solution creates value for the customer without disturbances. Cummins Engines leases uptime for trucks; GE jet engines similarly sell uptime or power by the hour. Such solutions encompass more than just the actual products.

Underlying reasons for the development of solutions such as uptime is the decrease in product profitability and that the installed base of physical products has altered the customer's value-creation processes. Installed base refers to the amount of physical products in existence that the customers are using. In a mature market, the customer already has the desired goods, for example, equipment and machines, and is therefore more interested in securing efficiency and uptime. Increased competition lowers product prices due to competitors' offerings. Furthermore, the cost of purchasing a new good can represent one-fifth or less of the cost of peripheral services (fuel, insurances, repairs, and maintenance) purchased during the lifetime of the goods. Calculations show that the purchasing price of industrial goods is sometimes as low as 5 percent of the total costs of the total sum of purchasing, owning and using it. Obviously, firms are keen to offer services and acquire as much as possible the remaining 95 percent of potential revenue that a physical product generates during the lifetime. Therefore, service infusion results in the potential for new business opportunities.

In order to enable differentiation and get their share of the life-time value of goods, many firms invest in a service portfolio, which means offering service in addition to the goods. Some examples of common services are spare parts as well as maintenance or service contracts. Some firms take it one step further, developing and providing a brand innovation, an experience innovation, or a process innovation, perhaps combined with business model innovation. The latter results in the transformation of goods into service platforms and experiences that can create customer value. Instead of emphasizing the good, the firm directs its attention to methods for solving customer problems. GE does not offer a jet engine, but rather "power by the hour"; mowing the lawn is no longer performed at specific intervals, but rather when the grass has reached a certain length; and firms have the ability to guarantee a certain improvement in productivity and get paid in relation to the success or failure of such endeavors.

Services can be categorized differently depending on the context, although a distinction is often made between services supporting a good and services supporting the customer (see Table 6.1). Services supporting a good are based on what the good requires in order to function, for example, spare parts, maintenance, or documentation, whereas services supporting the customer are based on value creation and focus on what the service provider can do to help the customer. Such efforts may involve sales of a function, improvement of customer processes, or taking over the responsibility for certain customer processes (process innovation). Assuming a greater responsibility for development of the customer processes can generate new revenue streams (although it has to be balanced against the increased risk) (business model innovation). It also requires the firm to think in new terms as it has to implement safeguard measures against physical product or service breakdowns, inability to deliver functions on time, and so on.

Using the physical product as a platform for value creation through services mandates changes in the technical characteristics in the good. Changing it leads to improved opportunities for value creation on the customer's part, which, in turn, potentially creates new revenue streams. For instance, increasing product reliability or modularity might be profitable as it potentially enables faster repairs. Whether or not such a change

Table 6.1 Services supporting the product and the customer

Services supporting the product	Services supporting the customer
The service is based on the product and the support needed for it to function well.	The service is based on the customer's creation of value and focuses on what the offering can do to help the customer's value-creation processes
For instance: spare parts, maintenance, and documentation.	For instance, sales of a function, improvement of customer processes, or taking over the responsibility for certain customer processes.

becomes profitable is governed by the firm's business model, that is, whether revenue is based on product uptime or downtime.

Viewing a physical product as a platform for value-creation challenges the existing business models of many firms, which may force them to develop new models or perhaps handle multiple ones simultaneously. A firm no longer regards services as a cost but, rather, as an additional revenue stream. The new business model then enables the transition from a goods logic to a service logic. The customers of the Swedish firm Tetra Pak include both customers who want to buy individual machines as well as those who would value a solution for the construction and maintenance of new factories. The business model to serve the former customer segment relies on optimizing the effectiveness and efficiency of the production process; in case of the latter customer segment, the business model shifts toward handling and optimizing service provision. One problem experienced by firms undergoing service infusion is that unsold goods can be stored and subsequently resold, whereas wasted working hours for service are impossible to store and bill later.

This shift in focus also applies to service firms such as banks and retailers. Many of them are entrenched in a certain type of goods logic in the same way that manufacturing firms are. Some organizations refer to their services as products and work according to the management principle "tangibilize the intangible." These firms attempt to *make* their services tangible and concrete, for instance, by packaging services as standard products, or having employee uniforms and tangible artifacts such as glossy brochures accompany all services.

An example of goods logic in a service industry is airports. The focus in a major airport seems to be on the airplanes and not on the customers' experiences. If it starts to snow, airport runways will be swept meticulously while the passengers are often left to wade through snow to get to the terminal. Sweeping the runway is vital and connected to safety; however, if the airports embraced service logic, they would also assist customers.

An example of service infusion is a cleaning firm that originally appeared on the market to sell vacuum cleaners to customers. The firm eventually revised its business model to provide cleaning services and then further revised it and offered to take over the responsibility for everything related to property maintenance. These services include cleaning, maintenance, air conditioning, security, and so on. Service infusion led the cleaning firm to offer solutions to meet customers' whole range of needs.

Service Infusion—A Process

Service infusion is a process without an end in which the firm constantly changes its offerings, organization, and interaction with customers. In some firms, goods still account for 95 to 100 percent of revenue. Even at traditional manufacturing firms where services now account for the majority of revenue, the physical products remain important. Without continuing to develop the goods side of the business, the service side can eventually disappear. Most firms are currently undergoing service infusion; the end of the process is not marked by a revenue based exclusively on services—rather, the position right for a specific firm is reached when it enjoys a balance between products and services that facilitates the customers' value-creation processes (see Figure 6.1).

It is not commonly known that Microsoft was first to launch a tablet, years ahead of Apple. Microsoft's initial offering saw its genesis as early as 2002; Apple did not follow until 2010 when it launched the iPad. When

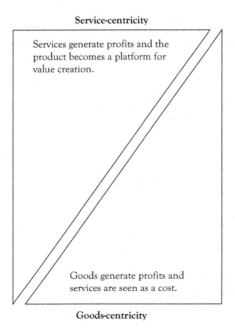

Figure 6.1 From goods-centricity toward service-centricity

Microsoft again launched its tablet in 2012 it was accused of copying Apple. How was Apple successful when Microsoft introduced the idea first? Much of Apple's success can probably be attributed to iTunes and the App Store: A customer wanted the service available on the tablet, not the device itself. The hardware is a platform that the customer is able to tailor to its needs. From a service infusion perspective, Microsoft erred by focusing on the physical product instead of its intended function, whereas Apple was more aware of the value-creation processes. Interestingly, it is possible to ascribe the failure of Apple's 1987 PDA or personal digital assistant, Newton, to the same phenomenon, as Apple had not yet created applications and services to facilitate its customers' value-creation processes; content is king.

A service infusion process must influence all levels of the firm. The strategic, tactical, and operative levels must all change—it cannot start and end in the management team. In order to succeed, a firm must be prepared to challenge its existing business models, offerings, customer relationships, and strategies. Of course, not all firms need to undergo service infusion. There will always be goods producers: Many of them will be located in low-cost countries.

Research studies have shown that, in the initial stages, a service infusion process requires additional resources and skills. It is expensive to establish an organizational structure and process primed to provide services. Firms must base their operations on what the customer needs, as opposed to only offering "new" products through additional channels. Services must fit customer needs, not just firm capabilities.

The biggest obstacles to service infusion are (1) corporate cultures not ready to become service oriented and (2) pricing new services. Service pricing is perceived as much more difficult than product pricing. The pricing of a service cannot solely be based on marginal costs—remember that a potential service cannot be held in inventory—service pricing should also take into account the value created by and for the customer. It may also be necessary to ensure that the customer realizes the value of the offering.

A firm we worked with described the difficulties it faced when charging the customer for productivity improvements in the customers' internal processes. The firm had improved the productivity of the customers' value-creation processes. Despite the productivity gains, heated discussions concerning what price to pay still occurred. The customer tracked how much time the supplier had spent on site, and felt it was fair to be charged a markup on the value of the employee time. Despite agreeing beforehand to split the gains resulting from productivity improvements, the customer refused to pay for the actual value created, focusing on the amount of hours worked. The firm had used part of the customer's staff; so the customer felt that it had produced some of the productivity gains. One solution discovered by this particular firm was to become less transparent: The firm moved hardware and its employees off-site to avoid letting the customer gain insight into what kind of work they actually did and the amount of time spent.

The organization and accounting system of a firm producing goods are designed to support product operations. If the tradition is to provide services for free, it is natural to encounter initial skepticism from salespersons when asked to charge for services. It is quite common for commission and bonus plans to promote physical product sales, and then free services can be used as promotion. Some of the organizations we work with say that their salespersons would rather be involved in big business deals offering goods with a small profit margin than more frequent smaller deals with spare parts and services but with a larger profit margin.

For example, a firm that sells large machines has a 1 percent margin on a product that the firm basically only sells once to a customer while employing a 30 percent margin on services that customers need several times a year. Despite being common knowledge at the firm, it is very difficult to convince the salespersons to sell the services, instead of giving them away for cost or even free to sweeten a hardware sale. In reality, it might be better to give away the hardware and instead focus on charging for the services the customer needs in order to use it. Selling services is different from selling hardware and it is not uncommon that neither firms nor salespersons lack the foundation needed to sell services effectively. Goods customers are often not used to purchasing services, and traditional goods firms are not used to selling and providing services.

Many manufacturing firms talk about the importance of initiating a service infusion process. Some research indicates that services need to reach 20 to 30 percent of firm revenue in order for the service infusion investment to be truly profitable. The service revenue of many traditional industrial firms is significantly larger than that, often 30 to 40 percent of total revenue, which enables them to run a profitable service business. Service sales in goods firms is not a new concept, although it is attracting more attention both in Academia and practice than before.

The content of services given away by salespeople in goods firms varies, including evaluations, minor repairs or maintenance, or consulting. There might be additional services offered by different departments or individual salespersons. For instance, a local franchisee might host a children's party in its store as an addition to product sales. From the firm's perspective, this often involves offering customized and differently priced services that do not belong to a single brand. If the quality of the services is not on par with the core values of the brand, it may have a negative impact on the firm. If the children's party goes poorly, making them unhappy, parents will probably not become regular customers. Such situations are not viable if a firm wants to build a professional and sustainable service business.

The service infusion process can be described as a continuous process consisting of four phases (see Figure 6.2). The first step is to *identify* the services already offered by the firm, how they are marketed and priced, and what value they add for customers. Managers should ask themselves which of the offerings are important to establish customer relationships and which offerings have the potential to become profitable deals in a service business. This often leads to the discovery that firms already have a

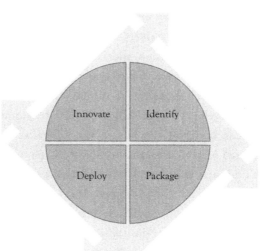

Figure 6.2 Development of an offering during a service infusion process

wide range of offerings, albeit scattered around the organization and not included in the strategy on how to grow the business.

In the second phase in Figure 6.2, the firm is supposed to *package* offerings in order to establish the service business based on the identification of the existing service offerings. Packaging involves identifying services that are provided in different parts of the firm and subsequently standardizing them to develop a range of services. It is advantageous to employ the service innovation process described in Chapter 4. Since some of the services already exist, it is not necessary to perform all activities in every phase—rather different methods can be used to package the offerings.

For certain services, it is the business model that needs changing and in other services it is new attributes that are needed to differentiate the offering. Packaging can also consist of building a new service brand (brand innovation), establishing a service organization, training employees, and identifying partners. When moving from a scattered to an integrated service range, services can easier be bundled to create new offerings. Maps can display how the services are put to practice and create value together with the customer. In Tetra Pak, a large part of the services have been standardized and sold through a service platform. By the same token, a number of SKF's services are offered under the service brand SKF Solution Factory. From having previously sold services based exclusively on a strong product brand, the firm has now begun to create its own service brand.

The third phase focuses on *deploying* the new offering: How should services be cocreated with customers in their business? This phase is the key to successful service infusion and transforms service logic from a theoretical concept to practice. Deploying a new offering may require employee training as well as changes to the organization and its network. Employees must develop a deeper knowledge of the customers, their processes, their needs, and how they create value. Services supporting the customer are based on close customer relationships, require knowledge of the customer's business, and assume the willingness and skills needed to improve the customer's value-creation processes.

The phase *innovate* involves analyzing the new offering to determine what is missing and, most importantly, discovering what is needed to work with service infusion. It is time to change the business goals and strategy, identify the opportunities of services, and create service innovations.

Innovations can be developed both within the boundaries of the product line or as part of a new range of services. Research has shown that a service logic or customer orientation, as discussed earlier, are needed for service innovation success.

A service logic might make it difficult to understand service innovation and to obtain funding for new service development projects. Succeeding with service innovation requires a service logic within the development organization and competence in terms of the customers' value creation, as well as a business model designed for services. This might require a new and separate process or even department solely with the purpose of new service development to prevent the services from drowning in the sea of product innovations.

A firm will not have completed its service infusion process in a single iteration through the four phases. Firms often discover new services from solving individual customer problems, which makes service infusion and even innovation a continuous process. If multiple customers need a solution to similar problems, the services need to be identified and packaged in order to become profitable. When a firm is in the initial stages of a service infusion process, focus lies on coordinating customized solutions. Over time, focus will shift toward creating an organization capable of providing standardized service solutions. Firms that prematurely focus on standardizing their services often incur undue costs, which prevent them from being able to establish a financially viable service business. Manufacturers like SKF and Tetra Pak then move into modularized service platform, since this enables them to standardize services to increase service productivity, but at the same time combine the modules in unique ways to customize the offering to each individual customer.

Service Strategies

One important aspect of service infusion through service innovation is to identify the role of each service in the firm's service strategy. Service strategy is determined both by internal and external factors. Internal factors such as resources, organizational structure, and existing products or offerings, and external factors such as the actions taken by competitors, customers, and other actors will affect the choice of strategy.

Stand-alone products can be sold in combination with either a maintenance contract or a performance guarantee (uptime). In reality, most firms have offerings that cover the entire range from product to service. However, in terms of organizational structure, the key is to find one design that can best provide the whole range of offerings. The service business is often based on the offerings that enjoy the highest sales volume. For instance, most suppliers of vehicles employ an aftermarket strategy as a large part of their revenue stems from spare parts and repair. A number of possible service strategies are summarized in Table 6.2.

For many goods-centric firms, information services, delivery services, and documentation represent the basics of their service activities. A customer service strategy means offering services in the initial product sales phase. Services affect customer satisfaction, increase customer understanding, and strengthen image of the firm. Each offering is based on the product's intrinsic value and ability to help customers create value on their own. The value for the customers consists of quality, price, and services that ensure product access. This strategy is often used when a firm initiates its service infusion process and is also best suited for firms that hold a strong product position on the market.

Being an aftersales service provider means providing spare parts, repairs, inspections, and training courses that ensure that the product is

Table 6.2 Overview of service strategies

Service strategy	Offering	Value
Customer service strategy	Information services, delivery services, documentation	Adding services in the sales phase
After-sales service provider	Spare parts, repairs, inspections	Product quality, price, response time in the event of product failure
Customer-support service provider	Preventive maintenance, repairs, inspections	Preventing product failure
Outsourcing partner	Taking over specific parts of the customer's processes	Decreasing the customers' capital ties as well as risk management and responsibility
Development partner	Developing products and systems	Access to supplier knowledge in the development phase
Brand developer	Creating new experiences, combining brands, promoting differentiation	Brand alteration in accordance with market opinions

working and used correctly. The goal is to be prepared to act as soon as a product breaks down. The business model is based on charging for reducing product failures during customer use. Value is built into both the product and the maintenance services of the installed base and it encapsulates quality, price, and response time in the event of product failure.

The strategic goal of the customer support service strategy is to prevent product failure during customer operations. The customer is offered advanced services such as preventive maintenance, process optimization, advanced operator training, and maintenance contracts. In addition to improving customer efficiency, the strategy focuses on the sales phase and the services connected to the customer's existing value-creation processes. This strategy relies on taking responsibility for customer relations, usually via a "key account manager," who follows the customer over time and develops a relationship by understanding the customer's needs. The general principle is to create value in collaboration with customers by customizing the offering. Some services that are suited for this strategy are presented in Table 6.3.

Table 6.3 Examples of customer-supporting services offered by Volvo Buses

Volvo bus vehicle management – Increase availability by optimizing service and maintenance Volvo bus vehicle management is an exclusively developed bus industry service. Its purpose is to achieve an availability as close to 100 percent as possible and to minimize every necessary repair service in terms of time and money. Every vehicle is given an individual service plan with optimized service intervals based on real-time data of the vehicle's actual usage and driving conditions.
Volvo fleet management – Optimize vehicle fleet productivity Fleet management is a real-time online service specially designed for the bus industry, which provides detailed operative vehicle information. Fuel consumption, emissions, and driver profile, as well as technical messages and events combined with geographical position are presented in clear reports.
Volvo traffic management – Real-time traffic flow management Volvo bus traffic management can be used for all types of public and private transport, for instance, scheduled and intercity services. Traffic management not only facilitates vehicle allocation, but also service monitoring and passenger information updates. The system analyzes and compares real-time data from all vehicles with the existing schedule and provides traffic management and updated information in terms of waiting times and delays to drivers and passengers.

Source: www.volvobuses.com/bus/sweden/sv-se/products_services/volvo_bus_telematics/Pages/volvo_bus_telematics.aspx. With permission from Volvo Buses.

Being an outsourcing partner means that the firm takes over parts of the customer's processes—the customer "outsources" parts of its production to its suppliers. The strategic goal for the supplier is to undertake responsibility for the customer's processes and thereby its risks. The principle is to reduce capital ties and take over all or part of the customer's risks. The customer is offered a reliable production service without having to invest the capital needed to establish a production facility. Value is generated jointly by understanding the customer's needs and requirements in terms of the production process and by constantly delivering on time. One interesting example is the Swedish firm ISS, which was founded as a security firm but now operates hotels and hotel processes, including caretaking, gardening, breakfast serving, restaurant cleaning, operation and maintenance of premises, conferences and events, property finances, window cleaning, property development, entrance mats, room service, coffee machines, fruit baskets, minibars, telephone services, vending machines, general furniture maintenance, luggage storage, outdoor environment, hygiene products, staffing, reception, and waste management for their customers. They support the customer in all value-creation processes connected to hotel operations. In a similar fashion, FedEx and UPS do not just deliver packages, but they can handle all aspects of distribution for firms, including warehousing, packing, shipping, tracking and delivering, as well as associated services like product repair.

Being a development partner means that the supplier offers to participate in, or take over responsibility for development work. The customers are given access to the supplier's knowledge, which also makes it more difficult for competitors to initiate sales efforts aimed at the customer. Small suppliers are often forced to carry out development projects without pay in order to deliver parts or systems to a new generation of products. Larger customers do not always want to pay for such services, which poses a challenge for the suppliers in terms of how to get paid for time and effort spent on development on the customer's behalf. ISS is again a good example, with its offer as a property developer, which means that it is able to engage in a firm by developing, for instance, a hotel property and managing property redevelopment projects. The firm then alters its customer relationship by changing position from an outsourcing partner to a development partner.

The final strategy is brand development, which means that a firm uses services to differentiate itself from other suppliers by providing the customers with a unique experience. One example is the Swedish retailer Ica Maxi's services that consist of charcuteries, fish counters, and bakeries. The firm also uses unique experiences where "the farmer's market" moves into the store for one week. In a similar fashion, cosmetic companies such as Lancôme and Estée Lauder hold short-term events in department stores focusing on certain products and bring professional comostologists to apply the products and train customers to use their products.

Another way of utilizing services for developing the brand is to create stand-along brand stores. Nike opened a "Niketown" store in Chicago over two decades ago to promote its brand: Niketown was a combination of a shrine to Michael Jordan and showcase for Nike products. There are now 28 of these stores, renamed Nike Chicago, Nike New York, and so on. As part of the remodeling and renaming of the stores, Nike said that they were now "*brand experience stores* aimed at giving consumers not only the gear they want but the service they seek." The stores emphasize the goods in use with videos and hiring athletes for assisting customers. Sony and Microsoft also have stand-alone brand stores, while Samsung has mini "Samsung experience stores" within Best Buy stores. The leader in brand stores is of course Apple Stores, famed for the "geniuses" and incredible sales per square foot measures.

Finally, some brands sponsor customer experiences and even communities. A leader at this approach is Harley Davidson. The company sponsors rallies, cookouts, conventions, and other events where enthusiasts can get together and company executives ride along with loyal customers.

In 1983, Harley-Davidson faced extinction. Twenty-five years later, the company boasted a top-50 global brand valued at $7.8 billion. Central to the company's turnaround, and to its subsequent success, was Harley's commitment to building a brand community: a group of ardent consumers organized around the lifestyle, activities, and ethos of the brand.[2]

---

[2] Fournier, S., and L. Lee. 2009. "Getting Brand Communities Right." *Harvard Business Review* 87, no. 4, pp. 105–11. (quote from page 105)

Harley "hogs" and "hogettes" do not simply buy a powerful, noisy, expensive motorcycle (as well as t-shirts, accessories, and lots of chrome), but they also join an active and very social community or subculture.

Different Ways to Start with Service Innovation

Being successful in one area is not sufficient to succeed in service innovation in a goods firm—rather, a number of different areas must be combined in the right way. Areas presented in Figure 6.3 are the offering, business model, technology, organization, and network. All areas are not necessarily equally critical for all service innovations. For instance, a firm may already have the competence and resources needed for service provision, thus obviating networks as means for service development and delivery. For other firms such as Antiphon however, the network could serve as the impetus for service infusion. Antiphon develops, manufactures, and markets acoustic products and materials. By establishing a network with the help of a consultant, Antiphon gained access to knowledge, skills, and resources required for providing a professional service it can sell to customers. The network became an enabler for modifying both the offering and business model. If all skills exist in-house, the right

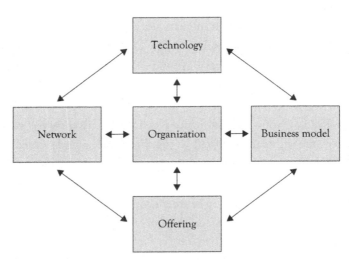

Figure 6.3 Different components needed for succeeding in service innovation in a goods-centric firm

organizational structure for service provision must be found, which might be difficult and it is not uncommon for firms to test various organizational structures before finding one that works. One common organizational change is to transform services into a separate business area with financial responsibilities.

New technology often works as an enabler for new services. Bundling information technology solutions with products makes it possible to collect data pertaining to product use, which can then be used either to develop the next generation of products or to sell services related to better using the products. These changes in offerings are often followed by business model innovation. Services that have been offered for free may now become the firm's main source of income. Volvo Construction Equipment's CareTrack system is such a service, which has made it possible to collect a large amount of data on customer use of haulers and excavators.

Developing Service Innovations in Goods Firms

Many traditional manufacturers seek to increase the share of revenues originating from services. It is not uncommon so see target figures of 50 percent of revenues or profits from services. However, the strategies, experience, work methods, and an organization primed for service innovation are often missing. Only a few people work with service innovation, leading to an organizational imbalance.

Our research shows that the average service innovation project comprises five individuals who work intensively for 9 to 12 months on a given launch. Comparing this to the development of new products illustrates vast differences. The most successful firms are those that have a systematic development process and continuously work to improve their services. Successful firms are seldom lucky—rather, they are skillful and learn from their mistakes—the gained knowledge enables continuous improvement. Our research shows that goods firms often suffer from two flaws in terms of service innovation: First, they lack a systematic development process for service innovation and second, an insufficient amount of resources is allocated to service development. In general, more than 90 percent of a firm's resources are focused on product development while service innovations have to cope with a paltry research-and-development budget. It is hard to imagine how goods firms can reach aggressive goals for value creation through services when the business only supports technological innovation.

A service development process does not guarantee success in service innovation. Research shows that one of the reasons is that numerous firms use processes and methods intended for new product development to develop services. In addition to not being adapted to the reality of service development, the development process often suffers from an excessive amount of phases and "gates," developed for incremental goods development. Instead of focusing on new service development, resources are used to get through a number of gates. In many cases, the service developer in a manufacturing firm can be viewed as an in-house entrepreneur that tries to build and grow a service business.

Market Validation: Innovation Lessons from Start-ups

One of the authors likes to sit in a local coffee shop near a new business incubation center and a well-known engineering school. He finds it enjoyable to eavesdrop on conversations and watch the figures and drawings go up on the whiteboards. From the terms being bandied about—"minimum viable product" (or "MVP"), "pivot," "iteration," and "market validation"—it is clear that new models of iterative innovation have caught the interest of the local entrepreneurs and aspiring entrepreneurs.

These models of entrepreneurial innovation are similar in many ways. All of the models stress iteration, getting user feedback by quickly going to market, being flexible, and running deliberate experiments. Adherents to these models seek to enhance speed to market, minimize financing needs, overcome the limitations of traditional marketing research methods, and benefit from real-time and full-context knowledge of users' value creation. Lean innovation is sometimes called "slow burn," while effectuation stresses affordable losses. These efforts are clearly compatible with the approach that has emerged from the discussion in this book.

The five iterative start-up innovation approaches (in assumed order of popularity by entrepreneurs) are:

1. Lean start-up[3,4] innovation;
2. Design Thinking[5] innovation;
3. A/B testing[6] innovation;
4. Agile[7] innovation; and
5. Effectuation[8] innovation.

Figure 6.4 illustrates the process for lean start-up innovation. The starting point is the MVP, which is the initial "experiment." After careful observation, data gathering and learning another experiment may make sense. If the knowledge points to a major change in the service, customers served, or the business model, the next iteration is called a "pivot"—as the company is now going in another direction.

Note that the four-step iteration after the initial MVP looks a lot like the experimentation or rapid prototyping suggested by Dr. von Hippel and Stefan Thomke. The lean process also has an uncanny similarity to

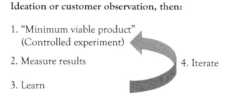

Ideation or customer observation, then:

1. "Minimum viable product" (Controlled experiment)

2. Measure results

3. Learn

4. Iterate

Figure 6.4 Lean start-up innovation (or experimentation)

[3] Ries, E. 2011. *The Lean Startup: How Today's Entrepreneurs Use Continuous Innovation to Create Radically Successful Businesses.* London, UK: Random House LLC.
[4] Blank, S. 2013. "Why the Lean Start-Up Changes Everything." *Harvard Business Review* 91, no. 5, pp. 63–72.
[5] Brown, T. 2008. "Design Thinking." *Harvard Business Review* 86, no. 6, p. 84.
[6] Christian, B. 2012. "The A/B Test: Inside the Technology that's Changing the Rules of Business." *Wired Magazine*, April 25.
[7] Highsmith, J., and A. Cockburn. 2001. "Agile Software Development: The Business of Innovation." *Computer* 34, no. 9, pp. 120–27.
[8] Sarasvathy, S.D. 2001. "Causation and Effectuation: Toward a Theoretical Shift from Economic Inevitability to Entrepreneurial Contingency." *Academy of Management Review* 26, no. 2, pp. 243–63.

the Probe and Learn[9] method of innovation that was observed in the late 1990s among high-tech equipment makers. The idea is to bring an "immature" product to market quickly and then follow the experimental method of Figure 6.4.

Design thinking innovation competes with lean innovation for the hearts and minds of innovative entrepreneurs. As already mentioned in our discussion of service innovation in Chapter 4, the three-step design thinking innovation process, inspiration–ideation–implementation, is similar to the focus, understand, and build process we observe in service innovation. The Stanford Design Center uses a five-step process for design thinking shown in Figure 6.5.

The other three processes are also iterative and experimental. Agile innovation is based on software development. It stresses continually working with users and not only starting with a simple version but striving to keep the software as simple as possible throughout the iterations and experiments. Effectuation innovation stresses the need of an entrepreneur to keep the "bet" on a radical innovation small enough that there are always other options available if experimentation shows that the innovation is not viable. A/B testing, based on development of websites, focuses on rapid continual experimentation.

Are these five Market Validation approaches to innovation consistent with the view of service innovation discussed in this book? Absolutely! In the case of radical service innovations, customers have a difficult time

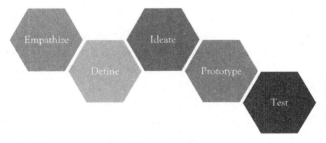

Figure 6.5 "Design thinking" innovation

Source: From the Design School of Stanford.

---

[9] Lynn, G., J.G. Morone, and A.S. Paulson. 1996. Marketing and Discontinuous Innovation: The Probe and Learn Process. *California Management Review* 38, no. 3.

giving feedback until they can touch and use a prototype, MVP, or immature product. All five of these innovation models stress getting market validation of the service and business model. Market validation is essentially deep feedback from the initial buyers (who will be some mixture of lead users and early adopters).

In the examples of lean and effectuation innovation, some of the ideas originate from a deep knowledge of the users' value-creation efforts, as we think ideal in service innovation. Market validation is a continuation of customer engagement, which we strongly endorse for service innovation. However, some lean and effectuation innovation projects originate from technological change or internal ideas, and the market validation is a search for a need. In these cases, the user input seems to be occurring later than ideal for service innovation. A/B testing is later stage customer engagement, consistent with our view of service innovation.

Design thinking innovation and agile innovation *explicitly* start with deep contextual user research, then go on to experiment with users, and collaborate with customers throughout the innovation process. Leading proponents of design thinking, the Stanford Design School and IDEO, both advocate observing users in context and the value of ethnographic research. Therefore, it seems fair to say that these processes are fully compatible with the principles of service innovation discussed in this book. Even though design thinking innovation originated largely for goods and agile for software, we would suggest that managers mapping out their organization's service innovation process look at the readings for design thinking along with our Figure 4.1 and select the phases that best fit your situation.

As shown, the new models of innovation for entrepreneurs are consistent best practices of service innovation. This should not be too surprising: As we noted early on, services are a growing part of the world economy and, increasingly, products are services even if a physical good is involved. All products are services; all marketing is service marketing; and all innovation is service innovation!

Market validation is another form of customer collaboration. It takes some advance planning to take advantage of insights from the initial buyers. Do you recall the example of the newspaper tabloid, *RedEye Chicago*, which was designed to be read on the subway trains? The initial version was pretty much a light version of the *Chicago Tribune*, the leading newspaper in the city. The developers anticipated that subway readers might want something different from simply a shorter version of the *Tribune*; so they planned for the early launch to be a continuation of the development process. Regular surveys were taken of customers on the subways and people were observed. New versions of the tabloid were tested several times a week. One of the leaders of the development work stated that the *RedEye* at the end of the early launch period was so different from the initial version that it was unrecognizable.

The smart service innovation team will work with users to plan for continued rapid development during the early launch of a new service. Of course, customer collaboration and innovation should never really end!

The entrepreneurial innovation processes can be used for service innovation in goods-centric firms. A key concern is to make sure that the project members feels familiar with the work practices. Research shows that the introduction of new work practices may actually reduce customer orientation if too much focus is placed on work practices rather than on the purpose of the new practices. A balance between new work practices and a structure that the project members are familiar with is required to succeed with service innovation in goods-centric firms.

Introducing Service Innovations

The service innovation process is not the only element that requires adaption; the way services are introduced to the market also needs to be changed. The development time for services is shorter compared to goods but their time to market is longer (see Figure 6.6). For a long time, Volvo Buses has emphasized the fact that the total development time of a new bus is identical to that of a new service for said bus; however, the ratio between development time and time to market is different.

The reason for the long time to market is primarily the time it takes to accumulate the capacity needed to provide the new service. Firms also want to avoid excessive capital ties and low utilization of the capacity for service provision. Services are often provided by personnel through activities that are interlinked and, in addition, linked to physical products. In the event of a service launch, technicians and sales managers have to be

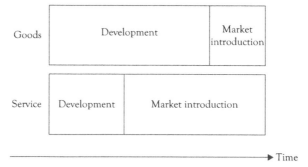

Figure 6.6 Development and market introduction—a complex interplay

trained in order to handle service provision, and for goods-centric firms, the time required to successfully train staff on their capability for service provision should not be underestimated.

Goods logic makes the staff into heroes when fixing problems, handling emergencies such as repairing machines on-site or starting a production line that does not run. As one manager said "Nobody ever gets credit for fixing the problem that never happened." Service logic, on the other hand, involves guaranteeing productivity through well-planned preventive maintenance that obviates machine repairs altogether—the fewer the repairs required, the higher the success rate and revenues. The era of the traditional hero has been replaced by the person seated by a computer, analyzing production data while making recommendations to the customer in terms of optimal machine operation and maintenance. Customers want a hassle-free ownership experience and are not willing to spend time solving problems they have not caused.

One additional factor that must be taken into account when estimating time to market is that a goods firm's presence on the market differs between markets. The value networks needed to provide services simply look different between markets. In service infusion, capacity for service provision must be accumulated and the service itself must be adapted to the presence and value network peculiar to each market. It is not uncommon to find multiple market channels at each market—one such example is retail firms that sell products in specialized concept stores, other store chains and e-shops, or via direct sales at events and exhibitions. This is a complex situation and the challenge lies in how the firm can offer the same experience regardless of the market channel chosen by the customer.

Services—A Cost or a Profitable Business?

Introducing services in goods-centric firms often involves assigning a key role to a previously uninteresting area viewed as a cost center. Services that have been offered for free are now supposed to become business areas that generate income. By tradition, the physical product is the arbiter of pricing, whereas services are given away for free in order to sell products (goods). This business model still works for some firms, but for others this business model is struggling.

It is often difficult to find a business model that allows firms to charge for services based on the value created for the customer. Why? One reason is the tradition of giving services away for free in order to sell physical products. This notion seems to be based on the principle that if a customer purchases an expensive product, it is only fair to make sure that he or she receives the training needed to use it properly. Another reason that services are too often cheap add-ons in manufacturing firms is the cost-plus pricing view—that the amount of work a firm puts in should correspond to the price paid by the customer. This way of doing business is deeply rooted in the practices of many sales managers and customers, which, in turn, makes the habits hard to break.

As noted, customers need training in complex products. A physical product needs to be maintained. If competitors have installed components on your machine that you know will not work as well as your own, you will obviously inform and perhaps educate the customer. All of a sudden you will start to give away a great deal of knowledge and skills for free to ensure that a physical product that was sold a long time ago keeps on working. Training, maintenance services, and consulting can be bundled with a physical product. A number of firms have begun to discover that significant value is given away to customers in a market suffering smaller product margins. The era of free services is over.

One additional troubling aspect is that engineers, salespersons, or both might not be inspired to develop and sell a cleaning or maintenance contract when they are accustomed to selling capital-intensive machines.

These machines, despite being a huge expense on the customer's part, often only have a very small profit margin. Such a big business deal is probably only carried out once, while negotiations of maintenance contracts, which are sometimes given away for free, take place more often and offer a much higher margin. In addition, some services are developed solely because of firm capabilities, not because customer needs them. Such services are obviously hard to sell. There is often immaturity among suppliers and customers in terms of service appraisal and pricing, especially early in the service infusion process.

Pricing paradoxes are evident on the Internet. How is it that news in the paper editions of most local newspapers cost money while the same content is often available for free online? Arguably, the online version should be more valuable since it can be consumed anytime on multiple devices. Tradition stipulates that a newspaper in its paper edition has to cost money while information online should be provided and consumed for free. Too often services generate costs while firms hope to make them up through profits on a physical product.

Finding a new business model is, as indicated earlier, a difficult challenge for a goods firm. It is also not sufficient to develop the right business model—it has to be modified in the right way and the organization has to be adapted to it. This process can be summarized in three core components:

- Find the right business and payment model.
- Change the organization from providing services for free to services for fee.
- Adapt the organization to ensure provision of professional services.

Today, the business model canvas has gradually become the de facto tool for the development of new business models. A canvas consists of a blank sheet of paper on which a new business model based on a number of key areas such as partners, resources, offerings, channels, customers, costs, and payment streams are supposed to be sketched out.

Let us use coffee as an example for the business canvas—coffee, designed as an offering today, is a product that is sold in vacuum sealed bags at a relatively low price per ounce. As a commodity, it has been exposed to fierce price competition, resulting in small margins. Customers however, have no problem with paying a high price to get access to the coffee in other places such as coffee shops discussed in Chapter 1. How then should coffee as an offering change from being sold at a price per ounce to something else? Coffee is a source of enjoyment, relaxation, stimulation, or a social lubricant. Coffee producers are actually operating in the relationship industry, which should be the basis of a new business model for coffee.

In recent years, an increasing number of people have begun talking about business models. The advantage of a canvas is that it works as a tool for quickly initiating discussions and ideas, although it does carry two big risks. First, the canvas should be applied at a general level and serve as the starting point in a journey toward a new business model. The journey does not end when a new idea for revenue streams has been created. Additionally, there is a risk that the focus when developing a new business model becomes excessively resource focused, thus sidelining the value creation in the customer's context. We feel that the nature of the customer's value creation should be the starting point for the business model. If used in the right way, the business model canvas is an excellent tool for service innovation.

Changing from one business model to another can be regarded as simple—after all, is it not just a case of changing the way customers are charged? Customers might have an equally simple answer—why not just change suppliers? In our studies, we have discovered several ways of changing business models. The simplest strategy is based on changing the business model of the firm's entire range of offerings. This is a dramatic change, especially if it leads to charging for services that previously have been provided for free. Customers may react strongly to such changes and will perhaps stop purchasing the firm's other products and services. If market competition is fierce, the supplier cannot assume that customers will return.

The other way of implementing a new business model is to modify the offering at the same time as the payment model. One example would be to improve the quality of the service or to make it more professional. Another alternative is to let the business model change apply to a limited number of offerings and, in effect, implement it gradually. Such a model reduces the risk of customer protests while also implementing the new business model change slowly.

The third way of changing business models is to involve a new value network for service provision. Introducing a new partner in an existing customer relationship makes it easier to carry out the change from service for free to service for fee. As such, the larger business model change makes it easier for customers to change the way they do business with their supplier.

The final key to success changing service for free to service for fee is to establish a professional organization for service provision. We have previously stressed the importance of the deployment phase in the service infusion process and it is worth repeating. Changing business models and creating greater value together with the customers also involve giving the employees the opportunity to develop in their new role. We usually speak in terms of employees being required to represent the service's soft values, the technological knowledge, and the brand. This poses a challenge, especially if the firm works with service infusion and thus changes the values of the brand.

Summary and Further Reading

Many firms follow a goods logic, which means that the corporate culture follows a goods logic characterized by a perception that the goods or standardized services are the key offering. Furthermore, such a firm is often blinded by the perception that their physical products or standardized services solve all of the customer's problems. Even though it is hard to believe, many traditional service firms operate in this goods-centric manner.

The basic principle among goods-centric firms is that they provide goods, or what we, in traditional terms, refer to as services (prepackaged or standardized), presented as offerings to customers. The customers are then expected to use the offering they have chosen in such a way that value is created. The antithesis of goods logic is service logic, where the focus instead lies on supporting customers in their value-creation processes by finding solutions to their problems or by helping them achieve their goals.

Services are facilitating the customers' use of certain products, which often function as platforms. Firms can also assume responsibility of parts of the customers' processes. We usually refer to the transition from goods to service orientation as service infusion. This chapter is intended to support firms that are facing a transition to focus on services.

Action questions for the service innovator:

- What services do your firm currently provide to customers?
- Which service strategy best describes your business?
- Is there a better service strategy for your organization?
- Which business models do you use? What alternative business models have you explored recently?
- Which of the services are free? Which do you charge for?
- Which free services could your firm charge for?

The main sources of inspiration for this chapter are:

Service infusion is a concept currently on the rise and the articles most frequently cited are:

Neu, W.A., and S.W. Brown. 2005. "Forming Successful Business-to-Business Services in Goods-Dominant Firms." *Journal of Service Research* 8, no. 1, pp. 3–17.

Oliva, R., and R. Kallenberg. 2003. "Managing the Transition from Products to Services." *International Journal of Service Industry Management* 14, no. 2, pp. 160–172.

Zeithaml, V.A., Brown, S.W., Bitner, M.J. and J. Salas. 2014 *Profiting from Services and Solutions*. New York: Business Expert Press.

Thoughts regarding business models have been popularized through the use of canvases to create and visualize new business models. Further information is available in:

Osterwalder, A., and Y. Pigneur. 2010. *Business Model Generation: A Handbook for Visionaries, Game Changers, and Challengers.* Hoboken, NJ: Wiley.

The ideas and concepts that we have been involved in establishing are documented in the following articles:

Gebauer, H., B. Edvardsson, A. Gustafsson, and L. Witell. 2010. "Match or Mismatch: Strategy-Structure Configurations in the Service Business of Manufacturing Firms." *Journal for Service Research* 13, no. 2, pp. 198–215.

Gebauer, H., A. Gustafsson, and L. Witell. 2011. "Competitive Advantage through Service Differentiation by Manufacturing Firms." *Journal of Business Research* 64, pp. 1270–80.

Witell, L., and M. Löfgren. 2013. "From Service for Free to Service for Fee: Business Model Innovation in Manufacturing Firms." *Journal of Service Management* 24, no. 5, pp. 520–33.

CHAPTER 7

The Service Innovator—
Tying It All Together

Simplicity is the innovation of our time—innovations that simplify human life and creates a better and happier world.
                                        —The authors of this book

All products are services. All innovation is service innovation.
                                        —The authors of this book

In this book, we have drawn on recent research on service innovation and marketing, as well as the authors' experiences in observing, consulting, and leading service innovation, to provide a guide to this vital process. Research and experimentation by businesspeople, organizations, and academics are ongoing: We anticipate a need to update this project within a couple of years as more is learned. We believe that the previous six chapters contain useful information for (1) the innovator within a service firm, (2) the change agent in an organization that is undergoing service infusion, and (3) academics or consultants pursuing research in service innovation.

Major themes central to this project are briefly summarized in the following sections.

All Products Are Services

By traditional classifications, the GDP of most developed countries is 70 to 80 percent or more of services. This number would increase if the growing percentage of service sales by manufacturers ("service infusion" in traditional goods firms) is included. So even by traditional measures, "all products are services" is a reasonable generalization in Western economies. It is clearly absurd that most models and theories of new product development are based on producing goods.

In addition, the effort to be user centric and create a customer orientation in service and goods business drives the organization to focus on the "job" of the user—the value-creation process of the customer. From this perspective, the services, goods, knowledge, time, and other inputs are resources toward a service that a user needs: A drill aids in home decorating, a lawn mower aids in landscaping, and a car is a means for transportation. So it is not just the raw numbers: A theoretical approach also leads to "all products are service."

Goods manufacturers from IBM to Volvo are engaged in service infusion—increasing the sales of services and creating new services. As noted, a customer orientation—getting closer to users—naturally leads to a service logic view of the organization. In addition, firms are attracted to service infusion due to the attraction of obtaining a higher "share of wallet," as the initial price of a good is often a small percentage of the total cost of using it due to services such as training and education and maintenance. Finally, fear of commoditization and price competition with China and other developing nations drives firms to use services for differentiation.

For a more complete discussion of why all products are services, please review *Chapter 1*. For details about service infusion and service innovation within traditional goods manufacturing firms, reread *Chapter 6*.

Service Logic and Value Creation

Service logic and the resulting focus on the user value-creation process leads to an external focus for innovation. "Open Innovation" is not a novel concept to organizations driven by service logic; they seek to have outsiders, especially users and customers, involved in innovation of service.

Users and customers must be involved *throughout* the service innovation process. Since service innovation must be driven by the value-creation process, it is important to have input at the beginning of the effort. Investors must understand how customers currently use products, both goods and services, as part of their job and value creation and how improved products could make the process better. The only way to acquire this knowledge is to carefully observe and participate with customers and users while they employ the product and services in value creation.

Service logic inevitably leads to a more customer focus for new services. Fundamental changes or even new business models emerge from the service logic. Innovations can originate from ad hoc improvements for demanding customers. A discussion of innovation strategy contrasted streamlining or differentiating and problem solving or "experience." Once again the user experience is part of the service: If it can be meaningful or enjoyable, the service is enriched. Six categories of service innovation emerge from these strategic choices: process innovation, brand innovation, experience enhancement, social innovation, business model innovation, and behavioral innovation.

(Review a full discussion in Chapter 2.)

Service Innovation Process

Service innovation is different from new product development for goods. Service innovation is highly iterative and less structured than NPD for goods. Service innovation is so iterative that a rigid phase-and-gate approach will not work. The spirit of scientific inquiry and true experimentation is built into a good service innovation process.

Due to the flexibility and iterative nature of service innovation, the development time for service is often shorter than that for product innovation for goods. However, the implementation time for a new service is often longer than that for a good because of the necessary training of both employees and users on the new service. Organizations will experiment with a service innovation process in the same manner in which they experiment with an individual service innovation. A good service process will be externally driven and will involve customer and users early and throughout the process.

The authors present a focus, innovate, and build model of service innovation based on observation of successful service innovators. Design thinking proposes a three-phase process: inspiration, ideation, and implementation. Both of these models include a deep understanding of the customers, thorough knowledge of the value creation by users, and involve users throughout the innovation process.

The service innovation process is discussed in detail in *Chapter 4.*

Understanding Customer Needs and Empowering User Innovation

A deep understanding of customer needs and the value-creation process can only be obtained through direct observation and participation. Important customer knowledge cannot easily be shared as some of the learned processes are second nature and become contextual, tacit, or sticky knowledge that is not communicated even within an organization.

In order to uncover contextual information, the observer must be part of the context: viewing or participating in the value creation where it occurs. A set of proactive user research methods are better suited for this than the typical market research tools of standard surveys or group brainstorming and focus groups. Proactive research methods include site observation, voice of the customer (in-depth interviews on site), lead user engagement, experimentation, and ethnography.

To use proactive methods effectively and succeed in service innovation, a firm should cultivate a customer orientation. A study cited in Chapter 3 indicates that a significant amount of the variation in service innovation success can be predicted by just two factors—the organization's degree of customer orientation and use of proactive user research methods. To develop a customer orientation requires the dedication and persistence of senior management. A current research project also indicates that a type of leadership, authentic empowerment such as Servant Leadership, can lead to a customer orientation.

Customer ideas may be the best ones. Real experimental evidence is presented for the superiority of customer ideas. How does one solicit these ideas? Smart organizations search for innovations created by their users. Proactive tools that actively involve customers, including ethnography, lead users, experimentation, and—later in the process—market validation, are techniques to collect user input.

For more details on customer orientation and the variety of proactive user research methods, review *Chapter 3*. For a fuller explanation of the superiority of customer innovation and facilitating customer innovation go back to *Chapter 5*.

Go Forward and Innovate!

We believe that the preceding chapters present current ideas and practices of service innovation. We also believe that every employed reader of this book is in a service organization.

Apply these principles and ideas. Tailor processes and practices to your organization and its users' needs. Be proactive in customer research; involve users in service innovation. Go forward and innovate!

Index

OTHER TITLES IN OUR SERVICE SYSTEMS AND INNOVATIONS IN BUSINESS AND SOCIETY COLLECTION

Jim Spohrer, IBM and Haluk Demirkan, Arizona State University, Editors

- *Profiting From Services and Solutions: What Product-Centric Firms Need to Know* by Valarie A. Zeithaml, Stephen W. Brown and Mary Jo Bitner
- *People, Processes, Services, and Things: Using Services Innovation to Enable the Internet of Everything* by Hazim Dahir, Bil Dry, and Carlos Pignataro
- *Service Design and Delivery: How Design Thinking Can Innovate Business and Add Value to Society* by Toshiaki Kurokawa
- *All Services, All the Time: How Business Services Serve Your Business* by Doug McDavid
- *Modeling Service Systems* by Ralph Badinelli
- *Obtaining Value from Big Data for Service Delivery* by Stephen H. Kaisler, Frank Armour, J. Alberto Espinosa, and William Money

Announcing the Business Expert Press Digital Library

Concise e-books business students need for classroom and research

This book can also be purchased in an e-book collection by your library as

- a one-time purchase,
- that is owned forever,
- allows for simultaneous readers,
- has no restrictions on printing, and
- can be downloaded as PDFs from within the library community.

Our digital library collections are a great solution to beat the rising cost of textbooks. E-books can be loaded into their course management systems or onto students' e-book readers.
The **Business Expert Press** digital libraries are very affordable, with no obligation to buy in future years. For more information, please visit **www.businessexpertpress.com/librarians**. To set up a trial in the United States, please email **sales@businessexpertpress.com**.

CPSIA information can be obtained
at www.ICGtesting.com
Printed in the USA
LVOW04s1632060716

495334LV00023B/945/P